# The Mystic Path
# to
# Cosmic Power

## Vernon Howard

New Life Foundation
www.anewlife.org

*For details on other Vernon Howard books,
audio and video and more, contact us at:*

New Life Foundation
PO Box 2230
Pine AZ 85544
(928) 476-3224
Fax: (928) 476-4743
E-mail: info@anewlife.org

ISBN 978-1-943362-42-4

Library of Congress
Catalog Card Number 66027957

# Contents

## A Cordial Invitation to You,

## the Reader: Learn Here

## What This Book Can Do for You

You may find this a strange and startling book. I hope you do. You may also find its principles a thrilling guide for transforming your life. It can do just that.

Who is the Mystic Path for? It is for men and women who are dissatisfied with things as they are, for those who hear a faint whisper that things can be entirely different. It is for anyone weary of the anxious ride on the Ferris Wheel of life that carries you to dizzy heights of elation and then drops you off right back where you started. Most of all, the Mystic Path is for those who are willing to challenge their present ideas about life — and change them when necessary.

People don't live the way they do because they like it. They live as they do because they don't know what else to do. The Mystic Path awakens that first faint hint of *another way to live*. It exists. I know it does. Anyone who wants this new life badly enough will find it. Then, everything alters itself dramatically. Just as a frozen river thaws with the warmth of spring, so does the new life flow freely and smoothly.

## What This Book Can Do for You

The individual who patiently and persistently walks the Mystic Path eventually rejoins his True Self, where daily life becomes amazingly easy. While one part of him may actively engage in the hurried worlds of commerce and society, another part stands serenely aside, bothered by nothing. Living from mystical principles, we find so little needs to be done or said. When a man tells a woman he loves her, nothing else need be said. That is how it is.

This book presents the great spiritual, psychological, and mystical truths in a simple manner, making them practical for daily use by the modern man and woman. The text includes numerous dialogues in the form of questions and answers. Over the years of writing and lecturing, I found them to be among the most often asked. They are intended to clarify and to encourage.

The Mystic Path is sunny. I want to emphasize that it is the way of genuine enthusiasm and lasting cheerfulness. So much awaits us! We finally learn why things happen to us as they do, which places us in control of our fortunes. Fear and tension vanish once and for all. No person and no circumstance can disturb our inner peace. Secret heartache is exposed and dissolved. We learn to love in a new way. Everything becomes right at last.

At this very moment, you, the reader, possess great capacities for miraculous self-enrichment. You need only exercise these powers as best you can. You need have no concern as to whether you are proceeding correctly or not. Just start.

Now we can adventure together along the Mystic Path. Just ahead is another life for you, brightly beautiful.

*Vernon Howard*

# 1

## The Greatest
## Secret
## on Earth

"What is the cause and cure of a man's or a woman's problems on earth?"

That is the foremost question ever formed in the human mind. Discovering the cause and applying the cure is the purpose of this book.

Mankind can be likened to a large party of tourists searching for a new homesite. They board a train that can take them from a dry and dreary desert to a grand and lofty mountaintop. The travel guide assures them that the higher they go, the greater their capacity to see and enjoy the countryside.

There are station stops all along the upward way. A tourist may get off and end his trip at any point he likes. He is perfectly free to cut himself short, or to continue all the way to the top.

Some get off at the first stop. They find themselves in desolate country. They settle down in secret despair.

Others go on for another station or two, then take their leave of the train. Their location is somewhat better, but, still, they settle down with a vague uneasiness.

A few others, the enduring ones, keep going. Somewhere along the early part of the journey, they made a fascinating discovery: Though the trip certainly has its challenges, the farther they go the easier it becomes. Patience and persistence present sure rewards. So they eagerly press on. As they do so, they reach the peaks of happy and unworried living. With enormous relief, they find that the mountaintop was not just something announced in the travel guide; it is real, it is there, it is theirs.

## The Needless Desperation of Man

Edward Arlington Robinson sums up the desperate predicament of man in his classic poem, *Richard Cory*. Everyone in town admired Richard Cory's princely manners. They envied his apparently exalted station in life. He seemed the very ideal of the successful individual. But it was all a stage performance. No one knew it better than Richard Cory. In his despair, he finally fled the stage in the only way he knew, in self-destruction.

Genuinely happy people are much rarer than one supposes. People wear a variety of masks: smiling masks, wise-appearing ones, excited ones, masks of worldly success, all in a frantic attempt to convince themselves and others that the act is real. But, sooner or later, the play must come to its end, leaving the actor alone and afraid on his little stage.

What does every man want? He only senses what he wants. He wants to be free. From what? From his heartache and suffering, from his compulsive desires, from his fear of what other people can do to him, from secret shames and guilts carried over from past folly.

He wants self-liberty. But he doesn't know what it is, or where to find it. Still, he anxiously seeks, and almost always in the wrong places. In despair over finding the right needle in the haystack, he doesn't even see he is searching in the wrong haystack.

He hopefully comforts himself, "Well, tomorrow will be different." But it won't. And he knows it. He knows he will look back and find himself in the same old despair. The only change will be in a few exterior surroundings. But it's still the same old haunted house.

The famous prisoners-in-the-cave allegory of Socrates, as told by Plato, explains man's condition: A number of men are chained in a dark cavern. A fire blazes around them, producing fearful shadows. Falsely assuming that the shadows are real, they cringe in terror and hostility.

But one prisoner gets tired of it all. Taking courage, he decides to risk all in an attempt to escape. Fighting his way through the darkness, he emerges into the sunlight of the real world. He finds himself a free man.

And what happens if he goes back to tell others of his wonderful discovery? What if he explains that their agonies result from their illusions, that an entirely new world exists on the outside? Will they welcome his message? They will not. What! — And give up their smug assumptions that they already know what is real? And disturb their ego-centered ways? No! They will scorn and resent him, call him a deluded fool — and remain in their secret despair.

What solution does the Mystic Path offer?

## There is a Way Out

Man is a frightened wanderer. That is an observable fact. But there is a second fact he rarely glimpses: *There is a way out.* It consists of finding his true identity. That is the only way any human being has ever shed the ache of separation, isolation, loneliness.

A prince was kidnapped at birth from his father's palace. Raised in poverty in a wretched village, he rebelled against the poverty of his life. He constructed careful plans for becoming king of the land. Through a series of schemes and battles, he won the throne. But he was anxious, hostile. Having taken the kingdom by force, he lived in dread of other ambitious men. It was day-to-day misery.

Then he learns his true identity. He is a king by birthright. He sees the folly of trying to retain by force what is already his inheritance. Now, with this kingly consciousness, there is no fear, no threat, only quiet dominion.

Observes Aldous Huxley:

> It is because we don't know who we are, because we are unaware that the Kingdom of Heaven is within us, that we behave in the generally silly, the often insane, the sometimes criminal ways that are so characteristically human. We are saved, we are liberated and enlightened, by perceiving the hitherto unperceived good that is already within us, by returning to our eternal ground and remaining where, without knowing it, we have always been.[1]

Every man is a king through conscious awareness of his true identity. He need not try to be anything; he need only realize who he really is — a king by birthright.

"How can we start practicing this idea?"

"How would you feel if you had no fear? Feel like that. How would you behave toward other people if you realized their powerlessness to hurt you? Behave like that. How would you react to so-called misfortune if you saw its inability to bother you? React like that. How would you think toward yourself if you knew you were really all right? Think like that."

These are kingly states of consciousness. By living with them, you live like a king.

---

[1] Aldous Huxley, *The Perennial Philosophy* (New York: Harper & Row, Publishers, Inc., 1945).

It is a fascinating process. A self-working individual will be sitting around home one day when the startling thought occurs, "Here I am, sitting around, doing nothing of interest, nothing to hope for, no one to talk with — and *I am not depressed.*"

He knows what would have happened a year or two ago in a similar situation. He would have trembled at the nothingness, at the lack of outside stimulation. But he has changed. He is no longer at the mercy of moods. He sees through the bluffs of negative impressions. He is quietly there. And that's all there is to it.

## The Greatest Secret on Earth!

What is it?

*By contacting a Higher Power, a man can live an entirely new life, both in the here and now and in the there and hereafter.*

That is the greatest secret on earth.

The Mystic Path leads upward to that new life.

How does the average man spend his day? He can be likened to a pendulum. Something favorable happens in his exterior life, perhaps a raise in pay, or a compliment. He feels good. But the next moment, strangely, the pay raise and the compliment become meaningless, so he swings over to depression. His entire day is spent wearily swinging from one state to its opposite — between confidence and fear, between cheeriness and gloom, calmness and nervousness, peace and anger, decision and indecision.

This is followed by feelings of futility, of being trapped. Though he may seek answers here and there, he has no real hope. Though believing that he may feel good tomorrow, he agonizes over the knowledge that he will plunge into emptiness the day after. He knows that his temporary elation will cruelly vanish, as the mirage disappears before the desert wanderer.

*There is another way to live.*

12

I assure you that this is no mere opinion of mine. I *know*. I also know that my telling of this can encourage but cannot convince you. But you can, by taking careful heed to the principles, convince yourself through actual experience. No person and no circumstance on earth can prevent you from experiencing the new life. Not even *you* can prevent it, if you are willing to change who you are. Our life-transformation is in exact proportion to the amount of truth we can take without running away.

What, then, is the requirement for the man or woman who wants to possess this greatest secret on earth? It is not strength, nor confidence, nor youthfulness, nor anything else like that. There is only one requirement: The seeker must be willing to listen, and to learn something new. With that, all things are possible.

Every man and woman, without exception, senses that there is *something else* beyond his ordinary life. The perfect evidence that there is something far better is his enduring search for it. Our task is to raise this unconscious sense to the conscious level where it enriches us, just as pearls enrich the man who brings them up from the ocean floor.

At this point, we can clear a major difficulty confronted by the sincere seeker. The moment he begins his quest, he is assaulted by the terrible thought that this too may be a delusion. He agonizes over the possibility that the answer may not really exist after all. His previous failures overwhelm him with the horror that this new reaching may also come back with empty hands.

No! If he persists, in spite of his doubts and failures, he will find the answer. It *exists*. The mystics have found it, and they point the way; but the discovery itself must be personal. So do this: Proceed courageously upon the principle that even just a glimpse of light leads to more light. For it always does. Just dare a lot, and you will get a lot.

"But all this may call for more of a spiritual life than I want."

"Don't try to be spiritual. That is only a word in the dictionary. Make it your goal to become a normally functioning individual. Let these principles shape you according to your real nature of a simple, decent, honest, unafraid human being."

"Then mysticism is a system for mental health."

"Of course. And much more."

## What is Mysticism?

We want to settle for an accurate definition of mysticism. As used and abused as the term is, we must clarify our thinking for the purposes of our study. We can state our definition in several different ways, realizing that they all describe the same essential thing. Mysticism is: **a.** An advanced state of inner enlightenment. **b.** Union with Reality. **c.** A state of genuinely satisfying success. **d.** Insight into an entirely new world of living. **e.** An intuitive grasp of Truth, above and beyond intellectual reasoning. **f.** A personal experience, in which we are happy and healthy human beings.

This describes *genuine* mysticism. Pseudo-mysticism seeks to evade reality; authentic mysticism wants to live it. Because it is real, it ultimately bears the fruits of love, understanding, and compassion within the individual. It has nothing to do with counterfeit claims resulting in individual turmoil and worldwide calamity. Fraudulent mysticism gives rise to self-deception, neurosis, unhealthy emotionalism. Our concern is with intelligence, normalcy, wholesomeness.

The authentic mystic is the sanest of sane men. Alfred Tennyson credits him with "absolute clearness of mind."

The Mystic Path is bright with cheer. Even if something goes wrong, the mystic-man remains peaceful.

He is like a perched bird who feels the branch give way.

14

Why worry? He has wings!

Is it philosophical, or psychological, or religious? It is all and none, for these are only verbal descriptions. It makes no difference what you label it, or whether you label it or not. Reality is beyond words. You can think of the Mystic Path as a spiritual journey, or as a practical experiment, or simply, as a means for a rich and purposeful life.

Some of the teachers and systems mentioned in this book represent the religious approach, such as Meister Eckhart and the New Testament. On the other hand, a Zen master instructs, "Stop wasting your time with theological speculations. Forget the fancy phrases that are supposed to indicate spirituality — whatever that word means. Get down to business with yourself. Find out why your life is such a mess and clear it away. Stop fooling around; get to the point."

## The Miraculous Message of Mysticism

No conflict exists between mysticism and the established religions any more than there is disagreement among several lecturers who describe the same sunrise. Only their presentations are different. William James, the giant among American psychologists, harmonizes religion and mysticism like this:

> ... personal religious experience has its roots and centre in mystical states of consciousness.... I think I shall at least succeed in convincing you of the reality of the states in question, and of the paramount importance of their function.[2]

All religions have produced enlightened men and women. One such mystic of India, Sri Ramakrishna, experimented by living, in turn, with various religions. He

---

[2] William James, *The Varieties of Religious Experience* (New York: Longmans, Green & Co., Inc., 1902).

was a Christian, then a Hindu, then a Buddhist. He discovered the same Truth in all.

Mysticism is not this or that particular cup on the table; it is the water poured into all of them.

It is enough to conclude that any man or woman who sincerely treads the Mystic Path in his own way will sooner or later meet that *something else* which is beyond definition.

What, then, is the miraculous message of mysticism?

*Happiness is yours in the here and now. The painful states of anxiety and loneliness are abolished permanently. Financial affairs are not financial problems. You are at ease with yourself. You are not at the mercy of unfulfilled cravings. Confusion is replaced with clarity. There is a relieving answer to every tormenting question. You possess a True Self. Something can be done about every unhappy condition. While living in the world you can be inwardly detached from its sorrows to live with personal peace and sanity.*

And this is what unknowing people call impractical mysticism!

This is the greatest secret on earth. Unfortunately, it is a secret hidden from the eyes of most men. But it is available to all. Anyone, who really wants it, can have it.

Never forget, you are following all this for your own sake. Your purpose along the Mystic Path is a very personal one. The objective of every seeker is to become an enlightened, happy, and pleasant human being.

## How to Perform Right Action

Millions of people assume it is enough to seek the Truth. It is not. It is essential to seek in the right way. The right way starts with a right frame of mind, with simple receptivity. *Everything depends upon the way we take the Truth.* No other mystical point is more important than this. The seed must fall on fertile, not rocky ground.

**The Greatest Secret on Earth**

The everyday mind misunderstands and distorts mystic principles. Non-action is a good example. Panicky people exclaim, "But we must *do* something. It's foolish to sit around with folded hands." This misses the point entirely. Mysticism explains that a panicky man is like a passenger on a reliable ocean liner. The passenger races furiously forward on the deck in order to get himself to port. If he would stop this panicky action, he would do the right thing, which is calmly see that he need not do anything but let the ship carry him to port.

Some inquirers are apt to think that mystic teachers dwell in some sort of ivory tower, having no contact with the realities of a harsh world. Such notions are quickly dispelled by reading about the early lives of teachers like Augustine and Count Tolstoy, whom we meet later. The difference between the mystic and his critic is this: The mystic has met and conquered the harsh world, while the skeptic is still punished by it. When a teacher is accused of knowing nothing about the everyday world, he reflects upon his own former business struggles, his affairs with women, and his own intensely hard work at self-liberation. When accused, he thinks of it all, smiles, and says nothing.

The Mystic Path has everything to do with everyday affairs. Take, as a single example, failure to break an unwanted habit. What goes wrong? The person fails because the very self who is trying to break the habit is the same self trapped by it. A man in this state is like a prisoner who dreams he is the guard with the keys. A new sense of self is needed. When the man discovers this new self, he also breaks the habit, for man's essential self is jailed by nothing.

## The Two Selves Within a Man

Certain basic principles form the foundation of the Mystic Path. One of them, which we now meet, will be referred to repeatedly. Your grasp of it makes everything else clear.

An individual lives with two conflicting selves within him: his True Self and his false self. It is difficult at the start to see that this is so, but what a fine first step toward wholeness!

The false self consists of *everything negative* within a person. Its nature is to be envious, helpless, angry, despairing, worried, critical, unstable, foolish, and everything else at enmity with happiness. Religions call the false self the devil or sinfulness; philosophy sees it as the lower nature; modern psychology calls it the ego-self that lives in illusion. But whatever the name, it is the cause of *all* inward pressure, which explodes outwardly in wars, crimes, and other social tragedies.

The man dominated by his false self does not *live* his day; he is *driven* through it. He is hounded by compulsive desires, pained by automatic angers, scared by unrealistic imaginations. Because he identifies with these terrors, that is, because he wrongly takes himself as his false self, his desperation is endless. He is clutched by an unseen enemy. "The entire root of your problem is that you cannot get out of yourself." (Francois Fénelon)

Now, it is utterly useless for a man to try to change or reform his old nature. You cannot improve it in any way whatsoever. *Here is where everyone makes his great mistake.* He thinks he can change his false self, which is impossible. The false self makes promises to itself which it can no more keep than a hawk can promise to change itself into a dove. "Of what use to make heroic vows of amendment, if the same old lawbreaker is to keep them?" (Ralph Waldo Emerson in *Experience*) It is the fixed nature of the false self to be negative, just as it is the nature of fire to be hot.

Then what can be done?

## Overcoming the Barrier to Happiness

The false nature cannot be, and need not be changed, but it can be dissolved and replaced by the True Self. Try

18

to see the difference in an impossible effort to change the false self and that of replacing it with your essential self. A hawk cannot be changed into a dove, but it can be replaced with a dove.

Remember, the false self is *false*; it is nonexistent, but, by believing in it, we act as if it were real. In reality, there is only one Self, one Power.

The True Self is, as the New Testament phrases it, the Kingdom of Heaven within. It is your higher self, the Divinity in man.

Now, since every man possesses this True Self, what are our possibilities once we release it through awareness of its existence? They are everything good and pleasant and satisfying. You can accept that as a fact right now, even if you do not feel it to be so. Forget your feelings; accept the fact.

> *I exist as I am — that is enough;*
> *If no other in the world be aware, I sit content*
> — Walt Whitman, *Song of Myself*

Our task is to dissolve the imaginary self and live from our real center of being. That is the only way to human health. But it is the sure cure. It is like removing a distorting blanket from a statue, enabling us to see its true form.

I find that the greatest single barrier to attaining this is man's secret assumption that he already knows the answers to his problems. But we all sense this pretense. Millions of unhappy people make this false assumption, but do not see it, thus freezing their potentialities for happiness.

A tremendous power works for the man who meets a challenging problem with the honest admission, "I don't know the answer." By turning his helplessness over to the power, he enables it to reveal the answer. It is like turning over the basic materials to a master rug-maker, knowing that he can take what we give and weave something far more beautiful than we could ever do.

Just as a subject under the influence of a stage magician doesn't realize his hypnotic state, neither does a man comprehend his life-hypnosis. And, of course, how can he know? While under hypnosis, he has no basis for comparison between hypnosis and wakefulness. Because the hypnotized man knows *only* hypnosis, he will scorn any other possibility. There is a way to break the spell, as we will see in following chapters.

## Finding Your True Self Changes Everything

Man has a false sense of identity. He thinks he is his false self, which he is not. He is his True Self, but doesn't know it. All man's grief can be traced back to his utterly vain attempt to prove this false sense of identity, for instance, through a compulsive drive to be admired and applauded. Yes, the egotistical self craves and demands applause, but man is not his ego-self.

The only evil is ignorance, unawareness, failure to see our authentic identity. To the degree that we learn to live from our true identity, our pains and follies fall away, to be replaced with peace and wisdom.

"But this is such a wicked world. I don't see how it is possible for an individual to live such a wonderful life."

"If you plant a tulip bulb in a weed patch it will still grow into a tulip."

Losing the false self is like this: Imagine yourself with an acquaintance whom you know very well but one who causes you nothing but trouble. You decide to put him out of your life, so he starts walking away. At first you feel anxious, for, as troublesome as he is, he is all you think you have. But then, something interesting happens. After your false friend has walked away in one direction, you sight a new figure in another direction. As the false friend walks away, to the same degree does this new figure come closer. Finally, you recognize him as a new and trustworthy friend, your True Self.

So the whole question is: How can we free ourselves from the false power of the old nature? Author P. D. Ouspensky quotes a modern mystic, George Gurdjieff.

Freedom, liberation, this must be the aim of man. To become free, to be liberated from slavery: this is what a man ought to strive for when be becomes even a little conscious of his position. There is nothing else for him, and nothing else is possible so long as he remains a slave both inwardly and outwardly. But he cannot cease to be a slave outwardly while he remains a slave inwardly. Therefore in order to become free, man must gain inner freedom.

The first reason for man's inner slavery is his ignorance, and above all, his ignorance of himself. Without self-knowledge, without understanding the working and functions of his machine, man cannot be free, he cannot govern himself and he will always remain a slave, and the plaything of the forces acting upon him.

This is why in all ancient teachings the first demand at the beginning of the way to liberation was: *"Know thyself."* [3]

Knowledge of his real nature. That is how a man achieves unshakeable success. He is like a permanent guest in a spacious mansion, who enjoys everything, while being responsible for nothing.

## Climb Aboard!

Whenever a new idea rushes into the mind, it smashes into a mass of distorting elements; like a ball tossed hard against the walls of a closet, the idea bounces against our fixed attitudes and opinions. In meeting the ideas of this book, you may find them bouncing against your present viewpoints. The new concepts may appear mysterious or

---

[3] P.D. Ouspensky, *In Search of the Miraculous* (New York: Harcourt, Brace & World, Inc., 1949).

illogical. When this happens, do not leap to automatic conclusions. This cuts off necessary inquiry. Rather, adventure with the new ideas, get acquainted with them. "There is a pleasure in the pathless woods." (George Gordon Byron)

Read as if you have no personal attitudes. Be open and receptive. This frees the mind of conditioned thinking, enabling it to absorb the new. We need start with nothing more than a simple desire to get the point. It is not a question of intelligence. Everyone has the intelligence. We need have no concern whether we are able to *do* this or that toward our inner happiness. Our only concern is whether we are willing to learn. And even if we are not, we can be willing to be willing.

The Truth at all costs! It is like an icebreaking ship that cracks its passage through frozen obstacles.

"But I get discouraged so easily."

"There is no need for discouragement over anything. Simply realize that you have not as yet grasped this or that idea. Why be dismayed just because you are in the fifth grade instead of the sixth? Keep studying. You are doing fine!"

On your first reading of this book, proceed without any particular effort to grasp anything that seems strange. Don't pause to puzzle too much. On your second reading, *do the very same thing*. But this time it will be different. Ideas which were previously vague, now sparkle. Already, they give you a new feeling toward yourself.

This chapter opened with mankind pictured as living at various levels along a railway. Ask yourself whether you are satisfied with your present level. If not, picture yourself as climbing aboard a new train. It is perfectly possible for you to be carried up the mountainside. There is a new train along every hour. Climb aboard!

## *Valuable review of Chapter 1*

1. Deeply within, every human being yearns for the free and enjoyable life.

2. The greatest secret on earth is that any man or woman can have this new life.

3. Your search for the richer way is perfect evidence of its existence.

4. The Mystic Path is a simple, sensible, and sure way toward all-around success.

5. You can find the answer to every problem and confusion.

6. Learn to seek Truth in the right way — with the fundamentals of mysticism.

7. We must dissolve the false self through right knowledge, and live from the True Self.

8. It is essential that we do not unconsciously assume that we already know the answers.

9. Adventure down the Mystic Path with a totally receptive mind.

10. Start right where you are.

# 2

# Wake Up
# to a World
# of Wonder

British novelist H. G. Wells was an explorer in the psychic world. An outcome of his search was the novel, *In the Days of the Comet*. This story has an interesting parallel to the fascinating subject of this chapter.

The novel tells of a world torn by warfare, intrigue, and treachery, in other words, a world much like our own. One day a mysterious comet approaches to hover over the earth. It discharges a great green cloud that puts everyone on earth into a strange sort of sleep.

Later, everyone wakes up. It is the same physical world, but what an amazing change has taken place in human beings. Hostility and mistrust are gone; everyone is calm and understanding. Soldiers climb out of their trenches to greet each other as friends. Peace is no longer a word, but an actual condition.

Awakened humanity realizes something previously unseen. Their wickedness was an outcome of their human-hypnosis. They saw that their previous platitudes, so noble and high-sounding at the time, were thin masquerades for selfish ambition. But all that had vanished. Now they see things as they really are. It is a glad and new world of wonder and happiness, like this:

> This life, this abiding, enduring peace that never fails, this serene power and unhurried conquest, inward conquest over ourselves, outward conquest over the world, is meant to be ours. It is a life that is freed from strain and anxiety and hurry, for something of the Cosmic Patience of God becomes ours.[1]

## The Strange Case of Hypnotized Humanity

Man is hypnotized. His entire life is one great nightmare, which he takes for reality. One of his handy sleeping pills is his blithe assumption that he is not asleep, that he is a perfectly conscious human being.

In spite of the repeated disasters occurring in his nightmare, he still insists he is awake. He goes through life like a sleepwalker, bumping into one painful object after another, but never letting the shock wake him up.

This is what the mystics have been trying to get over to humanity for centuries. "Let the pride of man be stilled; he thinks he is free but he is not." (Francois Fénelon)

Man is in a *peculiar kind* of psychic sleep, which he fails to recognize. So he casually brushes it aside as having nothing to do with *his* life. Spiritual literature abounds with references to this unconscious slumber. "Awake thou that sleepest." (Ephesians 5:14) Remember, this was said to people running governments, doing business, raising families. These very people so busy in the material world are told they must wake up to a new sense of life!

---

[1] Thomas R. Kelly, *A Testament of Devotion* (New York: Harper & Row, Publishers, Inc., 1941).

We must not assume that we are spiritually awake. *This is of utmost importance.* We have already seen that one of the smoothest tricks of the false self is to deceive us into thinking that our present state, even when filled with charitable activities, is a conscious one. No, we must proceed with the idea that we are presently hypnotized. It helps to understand that this is a *different kind* of psychic slumber, which we don't recognize as yet.

Another great help is to see that alertness in exterior affairs has no connection with psychic-awareness. Exterior abilities are on the mental plane; psychic skill is on a higher, spiritual level. This explains why a genius in politics, or science, or business can be utterly lost in his private life.

"You know, Mr. Howard, for a long time I have wondered what is wrong with myself and other people. The idea of a hypnotized humanity makes perfect sense. Why else would millions of people march off to senseless war? I hope we can continue with this subject next week. I want to know more."

"Don't be concerned if it is not clear to you just now. This merely indicates that you have not, as yet, escaped far enough to detect the difference between sleeping and awakened states. You see, a person in psychic slumber cannot possibly see what is meant by wakefulness until he actually wakes up. Suppose you are deeply asleep in your bed tonight. Would you hear someone who quietly informed you that you are asleep?"

"No. I see what you mean. To use another example, we are like canaries in a cage who have no idea of the open sky. But what a difference!"

"Awakening is the most *different* event a human being can experience."

## How to Wake Up to a World of Wonder

If a sleepwalker wants to stop bumping into things, what must he do? Wake up. That's all. Just wake up.

So must the man or woman in psychic sleep. He or she must open the eyes of understanding.

Having recognized, even dimly, the nightmare that keeps us weary and afraid, we want to end it. But how? How do we awaken from the bad dream?

A man must have a deep and sincere desire to change his inner self. He must be tired of merely rearranging the toy blocks of his exterior affairs and get down to adult business with himself.

With one man it is enough to feel a nagging dissatisfaction with things as they are. He is disappointed, restless, finding no lasting fulfillment in wealth, or fame, or social success. Another man might be jolted out of his complacent sleep by a shock, or a crisis, or by disgrace. When used as a message, not as a punishment, a shock can open a man's eyes.

A man must sense that something is wrong, deeply wrong. Now, every man has such a vague hint within, but he fails to listen to the message accompanying it.

This new and strange disturbance is accompanied by the ever-so-slight suggestion that there just might be a way out. He senses an alternative to his desperation, though, at this early stage, he has no idea of what it might be. It is a vague but entirely new hint of higher possibilities.

A few years previous to this mysterious stirring within, the man might have challenged a mystic, "Why should I bother with what you say? I'm a happy and active man."

"Because," replies the mystic, "you are not *really* happy — and no one knows it better than you. Beyond all your shallow pretenses and invented activities, you see your own emptiness. You can try to kid yourself, but you can't kid your nervousness, and your irritability, and your sleepless nights."

Now, having reached the end of his rope of egotism, no longer able to hide behind his pretenses, the man utters his first faint, "Yes, that is so. I am willing to go on from wherever I am to explore whatever there is."

## The Confession of a Famous Nobleman

This brings us to a man who woke up: Count Leo Tolstoy. Born into a family of nobility, Tolstoy was not religious in the usual sense. His early life proved the opposite. By his own confession he led a wretched life of robbery, sexual excess, drunkenness, cruel oppression of peasants, and violence of every description. As a soldier he was a vicious killer. Few crimes escaped him. So Tolstoy lived — and suffered inner torment. Was there, he faintly questioned, another way to live?

He began to write, motivated, he realized, by a driving desire for money and fame. He soon succeeded in attracting attention as a talented author. But it did nothing to cover up the inner agony. Looking around at his world he wrote, "It is now clear to me that between ourselves and the inhabitants of a madhouse there was no difference: at the time I only vaguely suspected this, and, like all madmen, thought all were mad except myself ...."

A series of journeys did nothing but heighten his horror of the human condition. He began to see what all seekers must eventually see with shock — the vast space between mankind's lofty pretensions of virtue and the subtle, self-seeking cruelness actually practiced.

But the psychic breaking point was near: "The truth was, that life was meaningless. Every day of life, every step in it, brought me, as it were, nearer the precipice, and I saw clearly that before me there was nothing but ruin. And to stop was impossible; to go back was impossible ...."

He searched frantically among all the established branches of knowledge. *Was* there a way out? His days were dark with the despair that it might not exist after all. The fear deepened when the scholars of the day had no satisfying answers to his inquiry, "Why am I living?" and

"How can I save myself?" Tolstoy's intense honesty compelled him to see that the learned men, who supposedly knew the answers, were just as secretly confused as he. In misery over the failure of his human reasoning to save him, he considered taking his life.

Then, gradually, the light dawned. From the New Testament he finally understood the cause of personal and mass wretchedness: "That men love darkness rather than light because their deeds are evil." Painfully seeing through his own deceit, he clearly saw it in others.

At the age of 58, self-liberation appeared. As the blindfold fell from his eyes, Tolstoy perfectly saw one monumental fact: Life is meaningful only when we are conscious — *really* conscious — of Truth, of Reality, of things as they are. We must wake up, be born again.

A free man, Tolstoy testified, "The light that then shone never left me again."

## Your Single Greatest Technique for Newness

We now come to the single most important technique on the Mystic Path. With its persistent practice, any human being can turn into a new person. This essential and dynamic technique is: *Self-Observation*.

Before we see what it is, we must see what it is not. I find many misconceptions here.

Self-Observation is definitely not self-centered mental absorption. If that could liberate, millions would be free! No, self-centered reflection is the exact opposite of genuine self-observation, and its worst enemy. Self-absorption is always characterized by uneasiness; Self-Observation is the method of destroying uneasiness.

Self-Observation is an act of watching everything that goes on, both within yourself, and outside. You do nothing but watch, just as if it were happening to someone else. You do not personalize. You do not react or form an opinion about anything you observe, whether it is a newspaper headline, or an inner feeling.

You judge nothing as good or bad, pleasurable or painful, favorable or unfavorable. You simply watch, just as if you have no personal connection with whatever you observe. Think of yourself as standing on a riverbank, watching passing ships. Some of the ships are bright with lights and color, others are dark and dreary; but what has either to do with you? You have no connection with either the brightness or dreariness — you are merely watching them come and go.

Self-Observation means passive detachment. You do not try to change the things you see in yourself; you interfere with nothing. Without attitude and without comment, you simply *look*.

It is a remarkable experience to stand aside and watch a fear, or a depression, or a passion pass through you without personalizing it. It is sheer magic that eventually changes things effortlessly and correctly.

"But I am thinking about myself all the time, anyway. I don't see any difference in what you say and my present self-preoccupation."

"We must be totally clear on this. Self-Observation is *not* thinking about yourself. There is a world of difference. Self-preoccupation is like grabbing and wrestling with a tiger. Self-Observation is like quietly watching the tiger walk by."

Why are we emphasizing this? *It is the very key to liberating self-knowledge.* It enables us to see ourselves as we really are, not as we imagine ourselves to be. Upon that realistic foundation, we build a new self; and, great news, when *we* are different, *things* are different.

P. D. Ouspensky quotes his teacher, George Gurdjieff:

Self-observation brings man to the realization of the necessity for self-change. And in observing himself a man notices that self-observation itself brings about certain changes in his inner processes. He begins to understand that self-observation is an instrument of self-change, a means of awakening. By observing himself he throws, as it were, a ray of light onto his inner processes which have hitherto worked in complete darkness. And under the influence of this light the processes themselves begin to change.[2]

## Try This Remarkable Experiment

When a prisoner-of-war plans an escape, what does he do? He observes the condition he is in. He becomes acquainted with the fencing, the schedule of the guards, and so on. Upon that intelligent information, he plans a successful escape. That is also our purpose — successful escape from the prison of psychic sleep.

Try it right now. Look up from this book. Shake your head to break your present mental state, and look around. Simply notice where you are. Don't just notice the room; *see also that you are in that room*. Think, "Well, I'm *here*." When done correctly, it gives you an entirely new sense of yourself. Do you see the *difference* in your thinking as you now look around the room and the state you were in a moment ago while absorbed in the book?

Notice this: While absorbed in your reading *you did not exist to yourself*. There was reading, but no conscious awareness that *you* were reading. But now, upon detachment from your concentrated reading, you are conscious of your own existence in the room. What a tremendous secret you have here!

We want to become self-aware human beings. This happens when we seek in the right place. "You men, why do you look without for that which is within you?" (Meister Eckhart) Awareness of the inner man is, as all mystics proclaim, the Kingdom of Heaven within. It is the Truth itself. *Awareness and happiness are exactly the same thing*.

Impartial Self-Observation is the gate to a new sense of self. It breaks through into the dawn.

---

[2] P. D. Ouspensky, *In Search of the Miraculous* (New York: Harcourt, Brace & World, Inc., 1949).

It is as if a savage from a remote jungle was taken to a merry-go-round at night and set upon one of the horses. He feels himself carried around and around but has no idea of what he is doing, or where he is going. He cringes at the surrounding shadows that seem to threaten him every time around. But as the light dawns, he understands. He sees the shadows as trees that, in reality, were never a threat. He realizes that not only is he now safe, but always was; he has only become aware of his security.

As the technique is practiced, we are bound to be a bit disturbed at what we see. We find we are not who we thought we were. We notice negativities we were perfectly sure were not within us. But we should not mind the disturbance; we should not turn away. We can take it. The new insight does not make us worse, as we might assume, but better. Why are we healthier than before? Because we have exposed to the light the very negativities that kept us unconscious prisoners. Psychic light, as any psychologist testifies, destroys darkness.

"Dwelling in the light, there is no occasion at all for stumbling, for all things are discovered in the light." That is the testimony of George Fox, the enlightened founder of the Society of Friends.

Nothing is more valuable to the prisoner who wants to escape than honest Self-Observation. So write down, memorize and work with this key:

*Impartial Self-Observation leads to self-awakening, which leads to self-liberty.*

## What the New Awakening Does for You

1. *Fresh health:* If anything is certain, it is that the awakening process ushers in a new era of health and vitality. It cannot be otherwise, for your dynamic psychic forces now work for your physical self, not against it.

2. *Freedom from nagging trivialities:* You experience great relief from unimportant things. You see that your *life itself* is much too vital for concern over being rich or poor, famous or unknown, fat or thin, popular or ignored, handsome or plain. They become as colorless pebbles surrounding a sparkling diamond.

3. *Lasting elation:* Can you think of anything more permanently elating than to know that you are on the right road at last?

4. *Loneliness vanishes:* Why are most people lonely, even when surrounded by a crowd? Because their sense of security is attached to its noise and excitement, which sooner or later fades away. The awakened man dwells in the world of his True Self, where loneliness is impossible.

5. *A new kind of self-acceptance:* Man no longer harbors a secret self-rejection. He is through with subconsciously labeling himself as stupid or wicked. He sees that such labels go with human hypnosis, but now awake, he no longer accuses himself.

6. *Wisdom in human relations:* A man in this new state, considering a business partnership, would wisely select men capable of mature judgment. A woman, contemplating marriage, would realize that it is a thousand times more important to meet a plain, but emotionally steady man than a handsome nut.

7. *Mysteries of life are solved:* The open-eyed man clearly understands the rightful place of sex, money, religion, happiness and so on. They are no longer problems. Each new insight adds another piece to the jigsaw puzzle.

8. *Personal safety:* Your five senses function efficiently. You see and hear clearly. Want to see a perfect example of how a self-absorbed state causes accidents? Watch the facial expressions of people as they cross a busy street. Most of them are a thousand miles away!

9. *Daily inspiration:* Just as a cup is open to everything above and closed to everything below, so is the liberated man. He receives a constant and fresh flow of quietness, cheerfulness, relaxation.

10. *Absence of self-defeat:* Ever notice what happens whenever you come across a misspelled word in a book? Your knowledge of spelling tells you something is wrong. You feel the urge to correct it. So does the liberated person correct his actions as he goes along. That is self-advancement.

11. *Enjoyment:* How many people do you know who really enjoy their day? The awakened man enjoys everything. If you ask him why, he replies, "Why *not?*"

12. *Everything becomes easier:* A space rocket takes extra effort to get off the ground, but finally reaches free flight. The awakened man floats forward easily.

## The Power of Self-Understanding

There are two basic methods by which one can grasp a practical self-knowledge:

1. Work with yourself.
2. Listen to those on a higher level.

In actual practice, these more or less overlap, but let's examine them separately.

You can work with yourself in the many ways already discussed. You can observe why you do what you do. A pain or problem can be tracked back to its origin in a false viewpoint. You can demand strict self-honesty from yourself.

But we should also avail ourselves of aid. Here is where the mystics extend their helpful hand. But this takes more heroism than might be suspected; for they are not going to tell us what we prefer to hear, but what we need to receive. We should humbly realize that it is ignorance of ourselves that places us in danger from ourselves. This is welcome news, for now we can break into the open.

If a man would put one-tenth of the energy he uses to defend himself into a program for finding himself, he would experience the miracle of self-change. Self-knowledge awakens us. If we are awake at the switch, we can turn our lives onto the right track.

Our responsibility is not to *do* anything but to *understand* something. Just as we can see more of the countryside from a mountain than from a hill, our actions emerge on the same level as the understanding that projects them. It is useless to try to act superior until the inner self is superior. It is of paramount importance to grasp this.

Self-knowing has nothing to do with college degrees, or book-facts, or public fame as a scholar. It is *self-insight*. Often, we must set aside our mental education, if we are to awaken our spiritual intuition. People ask whether it is really possible to transcend their own conditioned minds and contact a higher power. Swiss psychiatrist Carl Jung, who bridged the gap between Eastern mysticism and Western psychology, replies:

> To this question there is a positive answer only when the individual is willing to fulfill the demands of rigorous self-examination and self-knowledge. If he follows through his intention, he will not only discover some important truths about himself, but will also have gained a psychological advantage ... He will have set his hand, as it were, to a declaration of his own human dignity and taken the first step towards the foundations of his consciousness....[3]

## Nothing Can Prevent Your Richer Life

Self-knowledge is really a simple thing. It is getting to see how we operate, just as we learn how an automobile works. That places us in control of our human machine.

---

[3] C. G. Jung, *The Undiscovered Self* (Boston: Atlantic-Little, Brown and Company, 1958).

Insight into the two selves within a man clears up many confusions and contradictions. A mystic says that man is wicked. That is true. But he also proclaims the Kingdom of Heaven within. Also true. The True Self is everything good; the false self is all that is bad. A man's conflicts arise from the battle between the two. As we permit our essential nature to take rightful domination, we win. It was our understanding that preceded our victory.

Progress through self-insight is like a great disappearing act. Picture a man caught in the middle of a rioting mob. He is struck by fists and stones, whirled about, and cursed. But he has a magical potion for making himself invisible. Gradually, as he becomes less fleshly, the blows hurt less and less. Finally, as his physical self disappears completely, he cannot be hurt at all. Though he is still there as an observer, the blows pass right through him.

As our false notions disappear, nothing can hurt us. We see that we were hurt because of the ego-hardened self which takes everything as personal blows. But through self-insight, the hardness has melted, and with it, comes the quietness we always wanted.

"How will I know that I've grasped this idea?"

"You will know. You will no longer feel insults as insults, losses as losses, threats as threats. While other people may, on the human level, behave badly toward you, you are no longer on that level, so you cannot be offended."

This is the tremendous message of mysticism: You need not be hurt by anyone or anything; you need not be enslaved by anything outside you or within you. Not when you really understand.

Look very closely. You will see that no person and no circumstance can prevent you from becoming a self-understanding man or woman. Who is stopping you at this very moment? No one.

The Mystic Path never requires that you grasp more than you can at the present moment. If you can only listen to wisdom, then listen. If you can only understand that personal effort is necessary, then realize that much. If you can grasp just one truth out of a hundred, that is just fine. Do only what you can do for now. Progress is certain.

## How to Stop Hurting Yourself

Many people will not believe it when told how severely they hurt themselves by lack of self-understanding. They still wrongly think that harm originates from outside, rather than from its actual origin within.

Take negative reactions. Who is painfully negative when rain ruins the picnic — the rain or the reaction? Who gets hurt when someone breaks his promise to us — the broken promise or the person taking it with resentment?

It is as simple as this: We cannot cling to our negative emotions without paying the price. Can we be at peace at the same time that we feel frustrated? No. Can we enjoy ourselves while harboring dejection? Impossible. It is one or the other.

Suppose a man worked with this enlightening fact until he saw it clearly. He would at once drop his preference for negativity. He would see how it robs him of the very happiness he wants.

"I know the harm in anger, but can't seem to do anything about it."

"You can understand it. Anger flares up whenever something disturbs a pretentious picture we have of ourselves. The man, who sees himself as being important, will resent anything suggesting the opposite. If you don't try to be important, you cannot be disturbed. If you don't want to be an Indian chief, you are indifferent when someone takes your grand feathers."

The awakened man no longer commits crimes against himself, such as psychosomatic illness and a sense of shame. Shame is a crime against the self? Certainly. The born-again man sees too clearly into his psychic-self to fall victim to that folly. Not that he denies any harmful acts he may have committed against himself or against others, but he now sees why he acted like that — he was under the spell of his false self whose very nature is harmful.

Suppose a decent and sensible man is hypnotized by an evil magician and told that he is a fool. So he acts like one. But the next day he snaps the spell. Should he feel ashamed? No. *That would indicate that he still falsely identifies himself as a fool, which he is not. No!* He sees that his foolish behavior sprang from a false sense of identity. He doesn't condemn his past behavior; he understands it, which is quite another thing. His essential decency — which he always had — now commands him.

"The 'freedom' of the Cosmic Sense is supreme. It absolves a man from his former self and makes future slavery impossible." (Richard Maurice Bucke in *Cosmic Consciousness*)

Mysticism's declaration of independence can be summarized in just two words:

"Wake up!"

## *Basic principles that help you*

1. Mankind lives under a peculiar kind of hypnosis which he fails to recognize.

2. We can wake up to an entirely new world of wonder.

3. Count Leo Tolstoy is a good example showing how a man or woman can awaken to a new life of happiness.

4. Your single greatest technique for life-transformation is impartial Self-Observation. Use it.

5. Self-Observation is a quiet watchfulness of all that happens inside and outside yourself, without attitude or judgmcnt toward what you see.

6. By clearly seeing what we are like, we change ourselves into what we like.

7. Do not be disturbed at any negativities uncovered by Self-Observation. Your honest insight destroys them.

8. Remember all the rich rewards given to the awakened man.

9. Work for more and more self-understanding. It is a power beyond imagination.

10. Wake up!

# 3

# The Marvels
# of The
# Mystic Path

"But is the Mystic Path practical for modern men and women?"

"Nothing else *is* practical. You can prove it in five minutes. Just look around. Honestly, now, what do we see? We see heartache, defeat, quarreling, illness of every sort. Is *this* practical? It is entirely possible for any man or woman to live above all these defeats."

People also wonder how their attention to the inner life will affect their exterior affairs. They wrongly assume that their business, social, and domestic activities will somehow suffer.

They will do the exact opposite. They take on a brightness you cannot imagine. A new inner life always reflects itself outwardly. It is strange how people wrongly think in terms of either 'this' or 'that.' You don't lose one value by adding another.

A man with an automobile is given a boat. Does he lose the automobile? No, he has something *else*; another value. Both have their place and use.

The awakened man not only continues nicely with his exterior affairs but exerts a new command over them. Because he no longer uses them to feed ego-needs, he is totally free of worry. His sense of psychological survival does not depend upon this or that happening. In finding himself, he discovers a magnificent truth: *He is not at the mercy of anything in this world.*

"The man of inner life is easily aware of himself, since he is never totally absorbed in outward affairs. Therefore, his exterior occupations and necessary activities do not distract him, and he adjusts himself to things as they come. The man, whose inner life is well-ordered, is not bothered by strange and troublesome ways of others. A man is blocked and distracted by such things only as he permits himself to be."

What is more practical than this way of life, as outlined by the medieval teacher, Thomas à Kempis?

## How Good Things Happen to You

The time will come when you no longer try to make good things happen. They just happen. You will be astonished. You will be astonished, because you now see that whatever happens to you is good. Is this as yet a mystery to you? If words could only show you. Someday you will delightfully exclaim, "So *that's* it!"

We can take a modern situation to see how an aware man improves exterior affairs. A businessman can make this experiment: Before your next telephone call, or business conference, clarify its exact purpose. Write it down in a word or two on a slip of paper. Now, watch what happens. Notice the useless chatter. Be aware of how few people can get to the point and be done with it. By alertness to this wastage, you can take steps to save your time and energy.

It is not a question as to whether or not the Mystic Path is practical. A man must *realize* its effectiveness. So he must listen, absorb, probe, experiment. He must wake up to new possibilities. He must begin to see things as they are, not as he dreams they are.

If we look out the window during a storm, we see everything through the blur of the wet glass. The trees seem out of shape, the hills dark and vague. Yet we know this is only an appearance; they seem out of shape because of our temporarily distorted vision. When the storm passes, we see things clearly, as they really are, and *as they always were.*

Our life-observation starts with a collection of blurs. In our early confusion, we think we must change the trees and hills. But, as our vision clarifies, we see that we need pay no attention to anything out there. We need only to see them as they really are. *That* makes them right for us.

The moment a man utters his first faint "Yes" to his True Self, he begins to change his vision. It is the beginning of what all religions call the New Birth.

"Then we really can retain an inner quietness, while actively engaged in the turmoils of exterior life?"

"Perfect quietness. For one thing, the self-discovered man can be either a huge success in his outer affairs *or* a so-called dismal failure and be completely at ease."

## Anyone Can Enter The Mystical Life

"That's a new idea. How can a so-called failure be at ease?"

"Follow carefully. The self-free man has an entirely different concept of success and failure. In fact, the two terms don't exist for him. If success exists for him, so must failure, which keeps him nervous. Watch what happens to you, when you really grasp this. You will enjoy your worldly activities *regardless of results*. Have you noticed how concern with results keeps you jittery?"

"Now that you point it out, yes."

"Let's explore. In your new state of thinking, you do not use your worldly activities to give you a sense of self-esteem. You already know who you are, so you don't depend upon exterior successes to make you feel good. You enjoy *yourself,* regardless of results. You have no idea of the mountaintop feeling you possess when you no longer depend upon good results to make you feel good."

"I'd give anything to be unconcerned with whatever happens."

"Work with these ideas and you will be that way."

Anyone can enter the mystical life of inner quietness. Regardless of age, the clamors of business, the problems of his home, in spite of everything, anyone can enter. It is a matter of inner development. You carry your mind with you wherever you go, therefore, you always have the opportunity to work with yourself. Anxiety is in the mind; so is peace.

Yes, a simple self-contentment. That is a guaranteed marvel of the Mystic Path. You have no pressure to be anyone but whoever you are, a so-called success or a so-called failure. What a prize!

Diogenes was an early exponent of the contented life, the Henry David Thoreau of his day. Great crowds trudged from distant lands to hear Diogenes declare, "You lose the very life you seek when you wallow in stupid luxuries. You don't need nine-tenths of the things you scramble for. Don't be afraid to have nothing. Don't hesitate to be a nobody. Happiness is not what you have, but who you are. You are already exactly who you need to be. See it!"

True to his teachings, Diogenes was unimpressed by wealth and power. One day, when Alexander the Great visited Corinth, the masses flocked to hail him. Needing no hero to worship, Diogenes stayed home.

"Well," said Alexander, noting the absence of the

famous teacher, "I suppose I must go to him." The great warrior found the contented philosopher warming himself in the sunlight. Alexander asked the relaxed man, "What can I do for you?"

"Just one thing, please," replied Diogenes. "Stand aside. You are blocking my sunlight."

## Mysticism is a Personal Experience

The Mystic Path is a personal *experience*, not a mere discussion of ideas. Who wants to hear a description of a beautiful symphony, when he can feel the music for himself? No one is convinced of anything until he inwardly perceives that it is true. We can read about a spiritual precept, talk and reflect about it, but the final proof is internal witness. Then we *know*. If everyone else on the face of the earth disagreed, we would still stand securely upon the rock of inner illumination. "For the spiritual life is as much its own proof as the natural life, and needs no outward or foreign thing to bear witness to it." (William Law)

Mere knowledge is not enough. It must form a foundation for personal perception. Knowledge without insight is like a horse in a library. Knowledge of spiritual facts and the experiencing of those facts alternate as we go along. We study the recipe and then bake the cake.

As Alfred Tennyson phrases it:

> Let knowledge grow from more to more,
>   But more of reverence in us dwell;
> That mind and soul, according well,
>   May make one music as before.

Don't think that you must involve yourself with complex intellectual philosophies. Don't try to be profound or educated. That only wears you out. Just be simple. Let everyday life be your teacher.

*Everything* is useful for self-advancement. Look for more self-insight in the little things that happen to you every day. Ask why you reacted as you did to that unexpected news. Try to understand why you replied the way you did to a question. Be aware of the disappointment you feel when a hoped for event fails to appear. Waste nothing that happens to you. Don't resist anything; just observe it. This is exactly what the mystics do to reach the trouble-free life.

Does mysticism carry us up and away? Do we sight something out of this world? Dr. Paul Brunton replies:

> The only way to settle these questions is not by argument or discussion, but by *getting the direct experience* of divine illumination. And that is a personal thing. Each person must obtain it for himself or herself. Then only will you find out what is really meant by the kingdom of heaven. This attainment is not quite so hard as it seems to be, because you are not seeking something a hundred thousand miles distant; you are seeking something which is here — *right here* — inside yourself. You are not seeking something which is alien to you, but rather your own inmost nature, *your essence.*[1]

## Your Attractive Changes

A seeker came to his teacher to complain,"Master, I am unhappy with the people in my life. They are unfaithful, inconsiderate. I am not wanted or appreciated. How can I change them?"

Replied the teacher, "Change yourself."

The walk down the Mystic Path is toward self-change. If we reminded ourselves of this a dozen times a day, it would not be too much. We have dozens of arrows, like self-study and persistence, but we shoot them all toward the single target of inner transformation.

We do not seek a mere change in human opinions. That pins us down to the same level. The conditioned mind can

---

[1] Paul Brunton, *Discover Yourself* (New York: E. P. Dutton & Co., Inc., 1939).

only rearrange human ideas of the same limited value, just as you might change a dollar bill for ten dimes. But a gain in cosmic consciousness is like adding a block of gold to the original dollar.

Mystical truths uplift your level of consciousness. When it happens, you know that it has happened. How? What curiously attractive changes they are!

One sure sign is that you feel less flattered by flattery and less blamed by blame. An enlightened individual is affected by neither praise nor accusation, though he may get plenty of both from unawakened people.

Another pleasant change is an entirely new feeling toward time. You feel no sense of hurry, yet you accomplish your daily tasks far more efficiently. You live in that wonderful moment mysticism calls *Now*.

"In one of your books, you said that self-transformation frees us from a false sense of responsibility. Will you please describe this newness?"

"It is the only way to live. There is a certain aimlessness, a lack of concern, but it has nothing to do with common carelessness. You realize that all that furious rushing around the deck does absolutely nothing to move the boat forward. You finally grasped the Cosmic Truth that *the boat carries you; you don't carry the boat*. You sense that your abandonment of control does not mean disaster after all, but, for the first time, an enjoyable voyage. Before, you thought the boat would stop if you ceased pretending you were the captain. Now you know better. There is a real Captain. How glad you are to see it!"

## Men Who Have Walked The Mystic Path

The mystics themselves are a marvel of the Path. We have defined mysticism as a sane and practical approach to the richer life. So we can define a mystic as one who, having discovered this life for himself, points the way for others.

## The Marvels of the Mystic Path

The mystic *discovered* this new life. He once had every pain, temptation, and confusion as other seekers had, maybe a lot more. But he heroically sought and found answers. He recognized his self-deception and stopped it; he faced the horror of his illusion-based wickedness and dissolved it; he ran into one blank wall after another, but kept going.

The authentic mystic personally experiences the Truth; the hypnotized man merely repeats what he has been told. The mystic hears the music within himself; the unawakened person merely plays another man's phonograph record.

"Can anyone become a mystic?"

"Definitely. But please don't hold an imaginative picture of a mystic as some strange looking individual in a long robe. An authentic mystic is a sensible man who lives in the midst of a troubled world but is above its folly. A businessman at his desk or a homemaker at her stove can easily be a practicing mystic."

The great mystics of history possessed various backgrounds and personalities:

Lao-Tse was a librarian in charge of secret scrolls.

René Descartes was a lawyer, army officer, author, musician, psychologist, philosopher and a mathematical genius.

The Emperor of Rome, Marcus Aurelius, was caught between his love of the spiritual life and the demands of royalty. He wrote, "Look within. Within is your fountain of good."

Pythagoras, who lived about 550 B.C., used the principles of music to teach philosophic truths.

Brother Lawrence, whose real name was Nicholas Herman, was a big and awkward cook in a monastery. Though ignorant of literary matters, his inner victory expressed itself in one of the great mystical classics, *Practicing the Presence of God.*

Buddha was a prince who gladly gave up a kingdom in exchange for personal peace.

A champion on the athletic field was named Plato.

Danish mystic, Soren Kierkegaard, urged every man to be a rugged individualist in self-discovery. He made an amazing statement that could be said only by a man who had shattered his own false personality: "I have become myself."

But whatever their individualities, they agree whole-heartedly on the principles of the Mystic Path: **1.** Man suffers, because he lives under a peculiar kind of hypnosis. **2.** With right effort and knowledge, he can snap the spell to live anew.

It is as if you were traveling across the hot desert, stopping every so often for a drink of water. The first oasis-keeper might be a rough-looking character with a no-nonsense manner who bluntly waves you toward the pool. At the next stop you are greeted by a gentle personality who serves you with his own hands. Other oasis-keepers have their own appearance and manner, but all supply you from the same underground stream of water.

"Such men not only liberate themselves; they fill those they meet with a free mind." (Philo)

## The Courage of the Mystics

These teachers of mankind have more insight into human nature than a roomful of Sigmund Freuds. Having shed his personal ego, it no longer clouds the mystic's perception of things as they are. Most men are easily fooled by the shallow exterior manners of society; not so the enlightened man. He sees and speaks fearlessly of man's dreadfully destructive self-deception:

"Human life is thus only an endless illusion. Men deceive and flatter each other. No one speaks of us in our presence as he does when we are gone. Society is based on mutual hypocrisy." This is Pascal's blunt insight.

No, it is not pessimism speaking. It is the highest optimism and courage. A pessimist is one who refuses to face the fact of man's folly, including his own, because *he secretly fears there is no cure*. But the mystic *knows* that humanity's health can be regained. Consequently, he is unafraid of an honest diagnosis of the illness, seeing its necessity for the cure.

"I suppose we must face it. Most people stumble from one foolishness to another. Why?"

"Whenever someone does a foolish thing, he knows it is foolish. This creates a pressure, an anxiety, a sense of guilt. In an attempt to escape the pain, he behaves rashly again, but, since his inner nature remains unchanged between the two acts, the second act is also the outcome of a foolish nature. This creates another pressure and the next foolishness."

"How can he break the vicious circle?"

By grasping all that we talk about in these classes. You have nothing to do except become an aware man or woman. Incidentally, never feel ashamed or guilty over your foolishness — which does not mean you evade your responsibility for it. It means that you don't deepen the confusion as to who did it. The false self — which is not the real you — did it."

As you go through life you often make mistakes that cause you to cry in despair, "What's the matter with me? Why can't I behave normally, quietly, pleasantly?"

When this happens, as it does to everyone, don't fall into anguish. Use your mistakes, great or small, to see how they stem from a wrong sense of self. This gets you on the royal road once more.

## What You Should Know About Mystical Teachings

If the mystics denounce human folly with one voice, they offer deliverance with another. "All that pains you is only yourself, for you are at enmity with yourself," declares Jacob Boehme. But from the gospels come the gentle promise, "And you shall know the truth, and the truth shall make you free."

The persecution of those who see deeply into the human condition is a sad reflection upon man's aversion to life-liberating facts. When Dutch philosopher, Benedict Spinoza, refused a bribe of five hundred dollars a year in return for his silence, he was excommunicated and stabbed.

Jacob Boehme, the German shoemaker of Goerlitz, was denounced from the pulpit and hounded out of town by his own pastor, a self-righteous hypocrite named Gregorius Richter.

Immanuel Kant's charge that Christ's teachings had been set aside in favor of church ritual brought down upon his head the wrath of King Frederick of Prussia.

No one is qualified to judge a mystic except another mystic. A lower level of understanding cannot possibly evaluate a higher one. When a lower-level man tries to judge — which happens all the time — his judgment is like explaining the fruit of a tree while gazing at the trunk. A lower-level man fears those occupying the higher; the higher appears as a threat to his ego-centered concepts. We understand the person of a loftier level only when we reach that new plane for ourselves. Then, in a new humility, we smile patiently at our former foolish judgment.

To be of genuine help, a teacher must constantly urge the seeker toward self-change, which alone can liberate. The seeker must not be directed solely toward good works in his exterior life, for he will mistakenly assume that they are the same as inner transformation, which they are not.

It is not an easy task for the teacher, for the seeker persistently resists anything calling for the sacrifice of his frozen concepts. But the Truth must be told at all costs, no matter how unpopular it may be. The authentic spiritual leader, having freed himself of his own false need to be popular, tells the truth, whether it falls on fertile or stony ground. Such a teacher is the salt of the earth, though few know it.

"Do men of such profound perception exist in the world today?"

"Yes, and you can be very grateful for it. If you think the world is delirious as is, you would find it intolerable without their healing influence."

"What reassuring relief to sight such islands of sanity in a troubled sea."

## Understand This Vital Feature

We now come to a feature of the mind called *identification*. It is impossible to overestimate the value of understanding this psychological state, for it connects with everything in our lives.

Identification means that we mentally and emotionally lose ourselves in something inside or outside of us. We become absorbed in a person, a place, our career, a hobby, our personal viewpoints, almost anything. We lose our thoughts in these things in an attempt to feel secure. We hope to gain an idea of who we are; we want to cling to something that seems permanent.

But they give us no security; they create just the opposite. The moment we identify with anything, we become afraid of losing it. And since all things change, we get hurt when the object of our attachment is threatened, or when it goes away.

Identification also means wrongly to take something as being a part of our essential selves. Take your name. You are not your name. That is only a label attached at birth. If you change your name, it would not make *you* any different. Take the physical body. That is merely a vehicle for living on earth. Your True Self does not consist of name, body, money, home, career, a new hairdo, or your personal beliefs. *You* are something entirely different from these attachments, just as you are different from the clothes you put on in the morning.

We can certainly have a successful career and other externals, but we must not think they are part of the essential self. *Then and then only will we really enjoy our personal possessions*, for we will not fear their change or loss.

When we identify with our own thoughts, we call it daydreaming. We lose ourselves in thoughts about a thousand things — a plan for achievement, a remark from someone, food, sex, money. Notice this: Whenever you daydream, nothing exists outside of that self-absorbed state; you are unaware of yourself. You are not even aware that you are daydreaming; but a moment later, when your name is called, you snap out of it to return to the world. Losing ourselves in our own thoughts blocks the entrance of higher impressions that could strengthen us.

## How to Be Free of Sadness

Work with all this. One of your great gains will be freedom from the tyranny of sentimental memory. What does this mean? Watch your next arising of sadness. You will find that it connects in some way with remembrance of a past era that you consider more exciting, more romantic, or more rewarding than now.

This sadness comes from the unnecessary tyranny of sentimental memory and nothing else. The past gave us pleasure, but it is gone, and so we are sad. We want those pleasurable days back, but we know that all things change.

In your new and unattached state, you are no longer at the mercy of imaginative memory. There is no longer a painful yearning for what has been, but a gentle enjoyment of what now is.

Memory has its place in recording non-psychological facts, like the alphabet, but creates useless sorrow when misused in sentimental imagination.

A sure way to detect harmful identification is the pendulum test. Whenever we identify with anything we think is exciting, we sooner or later swing back to the opposite feeling of boredom. *Identification with excitement is always followed by an unhappy reaction.* Mrs. Jones has great fun at the party; next morning she feels depressed. Mr. Jones beams with joy over a big financial success; next day he despairingly wonders whether the only value in life is one financial success after another.

All this is not negative. It presents you with a wonderful opportunity to find lasting values in self-liberty. By ceasing to place our trust in anything outside our True Self, we cannot possibly be afraid of anything. This is the secret behind the mystical teaching that the man who has nothing has everything.

Marvelous rewards come to the non-attached man or woman. The boss may still be a tyrant, but no longer has he power to bother you. An irritating relative may be just as unbearable, but you are free of him. You, in your new role of a detached observer, are aware of everything but affected by nothing.

We have already seen that man's main identification is with his false self, his ego-self. He is not this counterfeit man, but his belief in it creates chaos.

If man is not his false self, who is he? He is his True Self, which is a point of awareness, which is an observer of all that happens. That is what is permanent and eternal in man.

All this explains why mysticism urges us to detach ourselves mentally. Lean on nothing outside your own spiritual self. Detachment never takes away anything beneficial; only the harmful.

## How to Walk The Mystic Path

Learning to walk confidently is largely an *unlearning* process. We must cease to accept the false as true. The degree of inharmony in our lives is the sure test as to the number of counterfeit coins we are taking as real. Increased consciousness gives us silver, not lead.

We cannot learn what is right if we secretly insist that we already know it. Now, this statement seems quite obvious; a man would quickly agree with it. Yet, there is something drastically wrong somewhere. If a man *truly* sees that he does not know rightness, his very emptiness leaves room for it, *which changes the man into a freer state*. If a man does *not* change, it means just one thing: he fearfully clings to the false assumption that he already knows rightness, which blocks entrance of genuine rightness.

Do not be afraid of your emptiness. It is not what you think it is. Do not give it false power by resisting it. Let it be there. Let it be there, if it wants, and you will see through a painful hoax played upon you. And then you will know something entirely new.

Think of yourself as erasing a mental blackboard. If we try to write new sentences over the old, it becomes unintelligible. We must erase first. Then, we write with clear wisdom.

Eagerness to learn indicates an individual's insight into his present helplessness. As stinging to the pride as it may be for the moment, he is on his way at last.

Mystical learning consists of more self-insight. Augustine received a flash of self-discernment while walking down a street in Milan, Italy. He saw a poor wanderer who was laughing and joking. Augustine reported, "And in truth he was joyous, I, anxious; he free from care, I full of alarms." Augustine painfully perceived that in spite of all his education and public honor he was far from possessing personal peace — the very peace he had urged others to find! But his honest appraisal changed things in his favor.

One interesting feature of mystical progress is that you take the whole business less and less grimly. At the start, a man is deeply serious because he has not as yet found any answers to his questions and wonders whether he ever will. But, with the dawning of light, he becomes cheerfully relaxed. Having caught sight of the harbor, he sails eagerly but restfully on.

## *Foremost features to remember*

1. Mystical truths make your life practical in an inspiringly new way.
2. Anyone can have the self-contented life. Sincere search is always rewarded.
3. Go beyond words. Make mysticism your personal experience.
4. Use every event as a source of self-understanding and self-advancement.
5. Self-change is a marvel of the Mystic Path.
6. The great mystics, having walked the Path successfully, now aid your journey forward.
7. Remember that, while exterior good works are commendable, they are not the same thing as inner transformation.
8. Spend extra time in studying the subject of identification. Then, don't identify!
9. Lean on nothing outside your True Self.
10. Walk the Mystic Path with relaxed good cheer.

# 4

# How to
# Feel Great
# Every Minute

Recently I was standing on a corner in downtown Los Angeles waiting to cross the street. The traffic signal suddenly went crazy, blinking senselessly from *stop* to *go*, *go* to *stop*. Confused pedestrians started, stopped, whirled around, started again. No one knew what to do.

That is what happens to people whose emotional signals are out of order. They just don't know what to do.

The entire secret of success with your emotions is this: *You feel good not because the world is right, but your world is right because you feel good.*

We start with that all-powerful principle of the Mystic Path: self-awareness. We must become acquainted with our emotional household; we must see our feelings as they actually are, not as we assume they are. This breaks their hypnotic and damaging hold on us. Negativities are like weeds in a deep basket. When we bring them to the surface of the basket — of our awareness — the winds of Reality carry them away.

Don't hesitate to challenge any negative feelings you discover within yourself. That is a giant step toward their dismissal. Over many years of lecturing and counseling, I find many people hesitant to question their negative condition. They fear there may not be an answer. But we must dare to ask anything and everything, especially when suspecting that the answer may be contrary to our present opinion. This gradually awakens the intuitive self which explains everything to us.

What a pleasure to hear someone frankly admit a confusion in order to clear it! Example:

"I don't understand. You say that emotional pains are caused by illusion. Illusion or not, I feel the pain!"

"A man certainly suffers from a frightening nightmare, but when he wakes up, where is the suffering?"

Whenever confronted by a particularly disturbing emotion, you may wonderingly inquire, "Is it really possible to arise above this?" With perfect assurance you may tell yourself, "Yes, even this."

## How to Understand Negative Emotions

Before reading this section, think of the negative emotion that bothers you the most. It might be boredom, restlessness, a sense of futility, something like that. This gives you maximum benefit from our exploration.

Grasp this basic fact about negative emotions: All arise from a false sense of identity. We think we are the false self, but *we* are not. *Every painful feeling* — sadness, envy, guilt, insecurity — is sour fruit of the false self. What a great day when we see this. We can destroy the sour fruit by chopping down the tree at its trunk. Then, how differently we greet each morning!

It helps to see that there is no such thing as a single

negativity in a man. The frightened person will also be defensive; the discouraged man will be nervous. Negativities are like marbles in a jar. Though they appear individually, they are all part of the self-enclosed ego-self. This is more good news, for as we crack the jar, away roll many negativities. Take hostility. Hostility is simply an aggressive expression of despair and heartache. When the heartache goes, so does hostility.

An obvious fact about negative feelings is often overlooked. They are caused by *us*, not by exterior happenings. An outside event presents the challenge, but *we* react to it. So we must attend to the way we take things, not to the things themselves. It is our happy responsibility to react constructively.

We destroy painful emotions by becoming fully conscious of them. We must see them clearly, without evasion, without any reaction whatsoever to whatever we see within ourselves.

"This seems to connect with the technique of impartial Self-Observation, which you speak about so often."

"Exactly. Passive self-examination brings negative feelings to the surface of awareness. We see them as being within us, which begins to destroy them. We become conscious of what was previously unconscious. Let's take an everyday example. Suppose you resent someone for pushing ahead of you at the check-out line at the grocery market. If you do not observe this resentment, you suffer from it unknown to yourself."

"It has happened!"

"But suppose you are an earnest student of the Mystic Path. On the way home you observe, 'You know, I was actually resentful. I really see it.' Now, you have stood apart from yourself and observed the resentment objectively. This clear recognition has already weakened the resentment, for you have seen it not as part of the real you, but as a hold-over from the old, habitual, conditioned self."

## The Mystic Path is for Heroes

Noticing our negativities is a curious process. It is like seeing a shadow and taking it as a frightening phantom. If you look closely, you see it as a mere shadow. But refusal to look at it perpetuates the painful illusion of a frightening phantom. This is the awful state unnecessarily endured by millions of unawake people. They suffer without knowing why.

My own early experiences show that advancement to a higher level of freedom is often triggered by a rebellion against the existing lower level. Simply stated, you get fed up with the pain of the lower level. You decide not to live that way any more. You get tired of enslavement to a habit. Everything you have done in the past fails to break the habit. So you dare to try a new way, such as understanding how and why habits are formed. That new understanding breaks the habit.

You must rebel constructively. Do not direct your rebellion against people or conditions, rather, against your own fear of people and conditions. Perhaps someone in your life bothers you. You need not get mad at him or her. But you need to say *silently* to this person and to yourself, "From this day on, I will no longer sacrifice my natural integrity to you. From now on I am living *my* life. I will no longer barter my true individuality in order to please you and to hold you. Take me or leave me, but you'll have to take me as I am."

When silently spoken with insight and without hostility, this speech begins a tremendous transformation within.

In his essay *Self-Reliance,* Ralph Waldo Emerson declares, "If you are true, but not in the same truth with me, cleave to your companions; I will seek my own. I do this not selfishly, but humbly and truly. However long we have dwelt in lies, now your interest, mine, and all men's, is to live in truth. Does this sound harsh today? You will soon love what is dictated by your nature as well as mine, and, if we follow the truth, it will bring us out safe at last."

The Mystic Path calls for heroes. To perform deeds of valor on the battlefield is not necessarily heroic. Authentic heroism is inner action, unseen and unapplauded by men. It consists in a willingness to wade, if necessary, through a thousand personal blunders in order to reach the next elevation. The basic heroism is an agreement to higher truth.

## How to Detach Distress

A story from Taoism tells of a carefree band of horses which galloped spiritedly around the hills and meadows. They dined on green grass and drank clear water from cool streams. Living freely and naturally, they lived contentedly.

Along came a famous horse-trainer named Polo. He captured the unsuspecting horses, declaring, "I know what is best for them." He bridled the horses, decorated them with cheap ornaments, gave them numbers. Then he made them perform in public. They were forced to trot about in precise formation to the crackling commands of a whip.

The once-carefree horses turned into mechanical performers — tired, sick, afraid.

That is how modern society regiments man. And that is why he is tired and afraid. How can we regain our natural and spontaneous feeling for life? Through the dynamic principles of the Mystic Path, like this startling one:

*You* have never been discouraged or depressed. *You* never have and never will make a mistake of any kind.

The clue is in the word *you*. As we have seen, man's whole difficulty lies in his false sense of identity. He wrongly takes himself as the negative false person. But, in reality, he is his True Self, which can no more be negative than an angel can be impure.

Here is how the mistake proceeds in a man's emotional

60

life: A feeling of sadness arises. The man immediately identifies with it, that is, he takes himself as the feeling. He thinks he *is* this feeling, which he is not. He doubles the error every time he says, "*I* am sad." The more he says it the sadder he feels; the sadder he feels the more he says it.

If you, the reader, run into this, what can you do?

Separate the way you *feel* from who you *really are*. *You* are not that feeling of sadness. Try to grasp this.

Impersonalize a negative feeling. Do not say "I" to it. Rather, refer to the feeling as "it." A man should say, "*It* is depressed, *it* feels helpless, *it* is enslaved by passion, *it* feels guilty, *it* craves alcohol, *it* wants revenge, *it* is terrified, *it* is a compulsive eater, *it* has heartache, *it* feels betrayed, *it* is confused, *it* does foolish things, *it* is secretly bitter, *it* is envious, *it* feels bored, *it* is nervous, *it* has sleepless nights, *it* is irritable, *it* is exhausted."

Do you see what this does? It separates the false you from the real you. By detaching this false sense of identity *you also detach the distress it creates.*

Separate your *feeling about yourself* from who you *really are* — a free person. Separate, separate, separate.

It is not an evasion of your responsibility when you attribute your negativities to "it." It is a new kind of self-responsibility, a genuine technique that delivers you once and for all.

Your whole duty is to understand this. It is your understanding that destroys painful negativities. Work with this miracle-method of the Mystic Path.

## The Cure for Depression

"My chief negative emotion is depression. What causes it?"

"Follow carefully. Your understanding rids you of the problem. Depression occurs when you catch a sudden insight into the emptiness of your life. A man thinks he is happy with all his business and social activities. But he catches a glimpse that it is all an act, which depresses him. It is like dreaming about a palace and waking up in a mud hut."

"And the cure?"

"Be willing to see through your pretensions of having a purposeful life. This is an awakening shock. But when we abandon a pseudo-purpose, when we have nothing left of the false self, a true purpose enters the life. Then, depression is absolutely impossible."

"I don't know what you mean by pseudo-purpose. There is nothing wrong about building a business, a career, or having a happy home."

"No, of course not. Go ahead and be a successful businessman, or homemaker, or whatever else you want on the worldly level. Be as outwardly prosperous as you like. But don't think it can add anything to your interior life. You must not use worldly success as a means of psychological identity, such as picturing yourself as an important person. This creates anxiety. Remember, you live in two worlds — the material world of business and homes, and the spiritual world. Keep each in its place. If you try to use exterior success to find your True Self, you will fail and fall into depression. You can't paint the outside of your house and expect the living room to look any different."

"Is this why successful people like movie stars often live so unhappily?"

"They get depressed because they catch a glimpse of their inner poverty. This frightens them, for they fear there is nothing besides this showy sham. There *is* something else. We find it by daring to abandon the false. Then, we have no problems whatsoever with our exterior affairs. This is what the New Testament means by seeking first the Kingdom of Heaven."

"But no one really pays attention, do they? That is why everyone suffers from depression."

"Work with these ideas so that *you* don't suffer."

Let's pause to inquire into the reason for our investigation of negative emotions. Why spend so much time discussing unhappiness? The reason is: it finally awakens us to the very life we seek. We cannot become happy by altering our exterior affairs any more than we can improve our handwriting by getting a new pen. The understanding of unhappiness brings happiness. To see what is false is also to see what is true.

We are exactly where we have chosen to be. But we belong where our original nature longs to be.

## Surprising Facts About Desire

The average man's day is characterized by strained efforts to fulfill inner desires through outer supplies. He is surprised and hurt when outer supplies are denied. He rarely suspects the base of the problem. He assumes that it lies in exterior availability, when it really resides in his own desire.

Mystical teachings about desire are frequently misunderstood. Those who read mystical literature are urged to be free of cravings. They react, "But my whole life centers around wanting things and going after them. What would I do without my desires?"

Mysticism explains, "No, do not try to extinguish all desires. But try to separate the healthy from unhealthy. How can you tell the difference? Watch them. Notice what they do to you. A false desire is painful, compulsive, nervous, angry. It keeps you running, but you don't know where. A false desire masquerades as real fruit, but it is artificial; it cannot satisfy hunger."

Healthy desires, mysticism continues, are quite different. They also activate you, but you run in a straight line, not in a circle. It is healthy to wish for greater self-understanding. It is just fine to desire a better life. It is healthy to yearn for the way out of your haunted house.

Freedom from compulsive desire is next door to heaven. How would you, the reader, feel right now if you were free from a certain craving? Do you see the magnificent possibilities?

If people involved themselves only with necessary things, they would, with one stroke, cut away ninety percent of their emotional griefs. But they mistake *wants* for *needs*. Genuine wants, such as for food, rest, recreation, create no problem. Being normal needs, they are easily satisfied. But false appetites, arising from the false self, keep the seeker anxious, even when obtained. One way to see a worthless goal as worthless is to obtain it. The child soon feels that he really didn't want the bee.

The identity of these needless cravings may surprise some people. You need not crave to be appreciated. It makes no difference whether you are popular or not. There is no need to lead the band.

If you could peer into your original nature, you would see that you haven't the slightest desire to lead the band, whether socially, commercially, or intellectually. Your inner self is quite content to remain in the ranks as a flutist or drummer. It is the ego-self that insists upon being the drum major. It is a sign of psychic expansion to be unconcerned with your position among the ranks of men. As long as we are spiritually in place, we don't give a hoot about our position in the earthly band. And that is when we enjoy the march and the music.

Every man senses the truth of this. But there is another part of him that dislikes the idea. This is merely the egotistical self which fearfully protests its threatened extinction. Good. Your task is to extinguish it.

Your True Self has no desperate or unfulfilled desires. It already has all it needs. Its very Self is what it needs.

## Your Freedom from Painful Craving

"Please explain how false desires cause distress."

"Let's track down a typical human trait, that of vanity. Have you ever noticed the undercurrent of pain and anxiety there is in vanity? We worry that people won't notice or appreciate us enough. Now, vanity feeds the false self, which has an endless appetite. It can never get enough; it keeps us chasing frantically around, seeking the food of attention and flattery. So observe how painful it is to live with this nagging offspring of the false self. That is a superb start for dismissing it from your mental household."

"Then the Mystic Path frees us from the painful desire for flattery and attention?"

"Trying to flatter a mystic is like praising an apple for creating itself. The mystic has extinguished identifications with his ego-self. He sees his own dependency upon a power far beyond himself. And so he has no worries in his human relations. He is not nagged by self-centered demands upon others. And that, incidentally, is a state of genuine love. You love someone only when you don't want something from him."

The lopping off of false desire provides amazing new command in your human relations. Other people have no power over you whatsoever. With full integrity, you face anyone with confidence. By not hungering for Mr. A's approval, you are free of him. By no longer needing Miss B. to dispel your loneliness, you are happy with her or without her.

There is only one real desire: to know what is true, to be spiritual. No more of materialism, no more of this egoism. I must become spiritual. Strong, intense, must be the desire. If a man's hands and feet were so tied that he could not move, and then if a burning piece of charcoal were placed on his body, he would struggle with all his power to throw it off. When I shall have that sort of

65

extreme desire, that restless struggle to throw off this burning world, then the time will have come for me to glimpse the Divine Truth.[1]

In summary, compulsive cravings are part of the artificial self. But as we awaken, they dry up because they no longer have a source. It is a wonderful experience to see them vanish forever. We are then left with healthy desires, in which there is no pain, and which serve our genuine interests.

## The Only Answer to Anger

A compassionate king wished to help the poor citizens of his land. He was also a wise king. He refused to hand out unearned benefits, knowing how they corrupt human nature. So he set up bountiful stores of food and clothing at one end of a long, dark valley. All along the trail he placed straw men, each one more fierce-looking than the last. The citizens who dared to face and pass by the fierce figures received their share of the reward.

That is what we must do. When faced with emotional barriers, we must become aware of their flimsy falseness. If we really do this, unwanted emotions level and disappear like a sand castle before the waves.

You eventually reach a very interesting state. You will have no time to fool around with things that used to bother you. You ignore them. You pass by. You smile in amusement at the childish attempts of fear and worry to drag you down. You calmly see that they have no power whatever to touch the new you.

In this advanced state, a businessman is not afraid of competition or poor commercial conditions. A wife is unafraid of her husband, or children, or relatives. A husband is without anxious feelings toward his employer

---

[1]*Vivekananda: The Yogas and Other Works*, edited by Swami Nikhilanianda (New York: Ramakrishna-Vivekananda Center, 1953).

or friend. A single person is no longer preyed upon by loneliness. A citizen is free of apprehension toward a domineering government or worldwide threats. On this higher level, no one is afraid of anyone.

"Then can men have no more power over us, because they can neither take us by our desires, nor by our fears." Do you see something of extraordinary depth in this declaration of Francois Fénelon?

"You know, Mr. Howard, I feel free in these classes to speak about things I usually hide. Take anger. I try not to get mad, but fail every time. I would like to hear what you have to say about this."

"You must stop trying not to get angry. This is suppression, which only makes it worse. Whenever you are angry, *be* angry, *without condemning yourself for it*. Listen carefully, please. You *do* condemn yourself for being angry; that is why you hide it. You have an ideal picture of yourself as being a peaceful person, a non-angry person. So, whenever anger arises over something, it shocks you. You are shocked because the actual anger clashes with the imaginary picture you have of being a non-angry person. Because you don't like giving up this flattering and phony picture, you get angry often."

"This is so utterly new. I want to think about it. So I must give up my pretentious picture of being a non-angry person?"

"You can do this by observing your anger without identifying with it. Simply watch it come and go, without shame or comment. This is the only way in the whole wide world you or any other person ever frees himself of anger. And it is quite necessary that you free yourself."

"Well, as you say, we can't be angry and happy at the same time."

## You Can Be Happy Right Now

Why does man feel so bad so often? What is wrong with our emotions?

Nothing wrong, says mysticism, that mental clarity cannot cure. The problem is man's insistence upon feeling a fact before establishing that feeling upon the foundation of reality. A psychological fact cannot be felt correctly until we first understand it. To place feeling before understanding is to cause tragic illusion.

We can be happy in the here and now. That is a fact. We rightly grasp this fact by seeing that happiness is a state of non-illusion, of seeing things as *they* are, not as *we* are. With this foundation, we feel happy permanently. But suppose we hear the fact and try to feel it without seeing what it means? In that case, the wild imagination projects all sorts of false ideas about happiness — for instance, that it comes through wealth or power. We may feel excitement at that, but sooner or later it collapses.

This is important enough to review: Do not try to feel a fact until it is personally understood. Do we try to feel the beauty of a symphony before reaching the concert hall? We must stop reaching for emotional sensations. They deceive. They prevent us from experiencing the fact which produces the genuine feeling. An emotion based on reality is permanent; it never fluctuates with exterior changes. A false feeling is as shaky as the mirage of an oasis. A genuine feeling comes spontaneously, when we sight a real oasis. This feeling cannot be shaken because the oasis itself cannot be shaken.

A tale from the Arabian Nights tells of Jallanar, a beautiful slave-girl. So impressed was the King of Persia by her loveliness that he took her into the royal palace as his queen. Although given every luxury by the King, she declined to speak to him. "Why," he asked, "do you not tell me your secrets? Who are you? Where do you come from? Why are you silent?"

Jallanar finally told him, "I am a princess, the daughter of a Sea King. I have remained silent in order to prove you. I now see that you are a kindly king who truly loves me."

The Truth is like that. Before giving us its joy, it tests our sincerity. When we are right, the right emotions come, and never go away.

"The most beautiful and most profound emotion we can experience is the sensation of the mystical." (Albert Einstein)

## Your Field of Diamonds

Remember this basic principle for happy feelings which were set down at the start of the chapter:

*You feel good not because the world is right, but your world is right because you feel good.*

Let's see how this happens. The following illustration is from my previous book, *PSYCHO-PICTOGRAPHY: The New Way to Use the Miracle Power of Your Mind.*

Suppose you are not feeling well one day, yet you accompany some friends on a leisurely drive through the beautiful countryside. Someone calls your attention to a lovely lake, but, because of your illness, you cannot give it your attention or interest. Someone else remarks about a magnificent mountain in the distance, but you hardly hear him. You pass one lovely scene after another, yet they have no meaning to you. Because your illness has taken all your energy, you have none to spare in enjoying yourself. It is the same to your mind as if these natural beauties didn't exist at all. In your present ill state, they have neither existence nor attraction.

But the next day you recover. You feel fine. There is no inward attention to anything; you are outward bound once more. So again you go on a drive; you visit the very same places. But now, everything is completely different. You enjoy the lovely lake and magnificent mountain. You respond to them. You enjoy yourself. How come? It was the very same scenery both times. But on the second trip *you* were different. You saw everything in an entirely new way. You had the inner freedom to see and appreciate your outer world. Like magic, your changed mental viewpoint changed the world for you.[2]

In Chapter 7 we will discover absolute evidence that our pains and difficulties are caused by distorted thinking. We will also learn how to correct the thinking and thereby abolish the pain forever.

Let me speak very personally with you, the reader, for a moment. If you continue working with all these ideas, absorb them as best you can, you will look back with deep gratitude for your persistence. How happy you will be that you kept walking. You will feel like a man turned loose in a field of diamonds!

Remember, every individual who has found personal peace and happiness, has been through everything you may now be experiencing. He or she knows the barriers and the frustrations you face along the way. He understands your concern over financial affairs; he knows how fervently you wish you had not made that impulsive error; he sees your secret sorrow. But this mystic-man knows something far above all this. He knows it can come to an end.

-------

[2] Vernon Howard, *PSYCHO-PICTOGRAPHY: The New Way to Use the Miracle Power of Your Mind* (West Nyack, N.Y.: Parker Publishing Co., 1965).

## *Vital aids to keep in mind*

1. Your world turns right when you feel right.

2. A clear understanding of negative emotions dismisses them. Work for their dismissal.

3. It is right and necessary to rebel constructively against tyrannical feelings within yourself.

4. There is not a single painful mood that you cannot separate from your life.

5. Use the techniques given for the release of depression. They work.

6. It is essential to gain awareness of the whole process of desire.

7. Your original nature, which can always be reclaimed, is totally free of painful cravings.

8. When we wake up to the facts of life, we are left with beneficial desires only.

9. Never condemn yourself for having negative emotions. Rather, find freedom through self-knowledge.

10. It is a fact — you can be happy in the here and now.

# 5

## Your Miraculous Source of Help

King Canute, the Danish ruler of England, was worshipped and flattered by his subjects. They thought he possessed supernatural powers which could keep them safe and happy. Being a wise monarch, Canute looked for a dramatic way to teach his subjects about the Higher Power.

One day, while visiting the seashore at Southampton, he ordered a chair be brought to him. When the puzzled attendants obeyed, the king commanded, "Set the chair in the sand, in the path of the incoming tide." As they did so, Canute sat down in the chair and asked, "Now, do you think the tide will obey me if I command it to stop? We shall see."

Canute commanded the tide to halt. It crept closer. He shouted the order once more. The tide advanced to splash around his ankles. The king continued his demands; the sea continued to splash against him with increasing force.

Finally, an impudent wave broke over the entire royal party, causing everyone to retreat, dripping wet.

"Now you see," King Canute merrily called out, "that the highest of human persuasion is as nothing when compared with Natural Laws. Do not seek to control Universal Truth, but ally yourself with it."

Today, in Southampton, Great Britain, a bronze tablet reads: *On this spot, in the year 1032, King Canute rebuked his courtiers.*

King Canute may not have realized it, but he dramatized the very message of mysticism: "Don't worship human beings. All human effort is egotistical and blundering. Don't hesitate to abandon so-called human power. Honestly, now, what has it done for you? There is a Higher Power. You may not realize it as yet, but there is something far above and beyond the human intellect. Let's search it out together."

## How to Contact Higher Power

In the deep corners of their minds people secretly ask, "Really, now, is there a Higher Power who can help me? I know that we all profess to believe in something far above our humanhood, but...well, quite frankly, why am I unable to contact this miraculous source of help?"

Yes, there is a Higher Power. Yes, man can make contact; and, if he could only see it, he has never been separated from it. In reality, we can no more be separated from Higher Power than one section of sky can be separated from another. All is One.

At this point, we can say that it makes no difference what term we use when referring to the miraculous source of help. The word is not the thing. We can use the terms God, Higher Power, Supreme Intelligence, Reality, Truth, whatever we like.

"I am utterly confused about Reality, or Truth, or whatever term we use. Can you help us identify it?"

"Do not try to identify Truth. If you do, your identifications will be based on your human desires and imaginations. This builds an unreal concept. And that, in turn, gets you into an endless mess of illusions and frustrations. Forget trying to identify Truth. Instead, work on yourself as outlined in these classes. Then, eventually, you will see that Truth is something entirely beyond mental concepts. It is not something you think about, as you might think about a beautiful meadow, but an actual experience; you are *within* that meadow."

Here is where man makes his mistake when seeking contact with Higher Power: He seeks it through his limited mental faculties. It cannot be done. The conditioned human mind can *think about, memorize, speculate,* even *believe,* but it cannot penetrate spiritual skies. Something far greater than mere thought is needed in order to *know.*

How can we know? Through *awareness,* which is quite a different thing than conditioned thought. We must become aware of the Kingdom of Heaven already within. That is why we are walking the Mystic Path.

It helps to remember the wise counsel of Meister Eckhart: "People should think less about what they ought to do and more about what they ought to be. If only their being were good, their works would shine forth brightly. Do not imagine that you can ground your salvation upon actions; it must rest upon what you *are.*"

## The Difference Between Thought and Awareness

Many years ago an East Prussian philosopher decided to write and lecture on the power of human logic and reason. To his astonishment he found that there was a wall beyond which human intellect could not pass. That startling discovery revolutionized his life. Reversing himself completely, he declared the existence of a Force completely unlike mind-power. He declared furthermore, that this mysterious Force is available to anyone who wants it badly enough. The seeker must be willing to seek beyond his limited mental forces.

That discovery was made by Immanuel Kant, giant among mystic-philosophers. It can also be your discovery.

Spiritual *awareness* and human *thought* are two entirely different things. We must never forget this. The human mind can begin the quest, but it cannot make the actual discovery of Reality. The human mind can raise the sail in order to begin the voyage, but, having done that, it can only (and need only) rest and let the winds of Reality carry it to port.

Now, while living on this earth, we need both spiritual awareness and human thought. The human mind, which consists of memorized data, is useful for remembering how to tend the garden, or figure finances, or greet someone in the morning. But awareness is far above mechanical memory; it is Reality itself.

Dr. Suzuki, the Zen master, explains:

The intellect raises the question, but fails to give it a satisfactory solution. This is in the nature of the intellect. The function of the intellect consists in leading the mind to a higher field of consciousness by proposing all sorts of questions which are beyond itself. The mystery is solved by living it, by seeing into its working, by actually experiencing the significance of life....[1]

This explains one of the great mysteries of life: How can someone who is brilliantly successful in public affairs be such an utter failure in his private life? For example, a wealthy businessman may be dominated by personal anxieties which cause domestic conflict. The answer is simple enough: There is no connection between his worldly success springing from the mental level, and spiritual skill arising from the True Self within. It is like

---

[1] Daisetz Teitaro Suzuki, *Mysticism: Christian and Buddhist* (New York: Harper & Row, Publishers, Inc., 1957).

oil and water which have their separate functions in an engine, but do not mix.

"Then what is the difference between a person whom we would call mentally mature and one who is spiritually aware?"

"A spiritually aware person is always mentally mature, but a mentally mature man is not necessarily an aware man. An individual on the lowest step of awareness is higher than someone on the highest step of intellectual maturity. The mentally mature man is ready to step up to higher consciousness. He has rid himself of enough mental junk to make room for greater insight."

Summary: Human thought races around the jungle in a frantic effort to find a way out. Spiritual awareness stands quietly on a hilltop overlooking the jungle, from which it clearly sees the way out.

## You Will Win!

How can we contact this purifying Higher Power? By lifting the veils of illusion that hang between the human mind and Reality. By seeing that the veils of the ego-self block the light. *By seeing this we penetrate into the innermost secret of human happiness, earthly and eternal.*

It is not the lofty sending station that is out of order; it is our receiving set. Somehow we cling to the notion that something is wrong up there. We are like a man with a broken television set complaining that the TV station won't send him pictures.

In his essay *Spiritual Laws,* Ralph Waldo Emerson sums up the mystical principle:

"A little consideration of what takes place around us every day would show us that a higher law than that of our will regulates events; that our painful labors are unnecessary and fruitless; that only in our easy, simple, spontaneous action are we strong.... Place yourself in the middle of the stream of power and wisdom which animates all whom it floats, and you are without effort impelled to truth, to right, and a perfect contentment."

It is only when we dare to float upon this stream of awareness that we really know that everything is just fine. It is a peculiarly contradictory state — we do not have the slightest idea of where we are going, and yet we are completely unafraid. "We feel and know that we are eternal." (Baruch Spinoza) *We know for sure that all is well.*

I want to speak to you with unreserved candor. Do you know what finally determines whether or not we find ourselves in the stream of wisdom and power? It is the way we take a truth that we don't want to hear. Anyone can run away, evade, pretend to accept, but this is not heroism and it is not genuine individuality. It is commonplace; it is what the mass of men and women do. That is why most people are far unhappier than they appear to be.

You see, all of us have degrees of resistance to the very truth that could save us. It is the very nature of the false self to resist and resent anything that threatens its tyranny. But if you are tired of paying the price, you can stop. You can be a genuine individual who refuses to run away from what appears to be a threat, but which is actually what you want more than anything else in life.

Stand up for yourself! You will win. Little by little, you will win. You may be reluctant to start because you are not sure what it is all about; you don't know whether all this makes sense. But it makes the only sense there is. So start.

Do not think that willingness to contact Higher Power must include the strength to do it. In fact, power comes only when we see our helplessness. We must see this unemotionally, simply as a fact, without shame or despair. This is what the New Testament means by losing our life in order to find it. Willingness does not mean strength; it means only a definite decision to change the direction of life.

## How to Favor Yourself

Success in life depends upon the headquarters from which we take orders. Picture a soldier on the battlefield between two military headquarters. To his left is the genuine headquarters, maintained by his own army. To his right is a counterfeit station, set up by the enemy to deceive him, to make him go wrong. His success depends upon his choice between the two.

We always receive accurate guidance from our genuine headquarters within. It is never wrong. The instructions may appear confusing at times; we may have difficulty in carrying them out, but we are good soldiers; we follow along. Sooner or later, falsehood must surrender to Truth.

The test of what you accept as true is the way you go through your day. Do not try to change your day; seek to alter what you accept as true. Then, effortlessly, your day will change in favor of yourself.

You need not understand everything in order to start favoring yourself. Start right where you are. You need not understand the secret process by which air refreshes the body; you need only to breathe. Likewise, live without worry or strain over the whole process of life. Here we meet one of those seeming contradictions which becomes quite clear after awhile: The less you strain your mind, the more it contacts the Higher Power that works through you and for you.

The soldier on the Mystic Path encounters many valuable challenges. One of them is a sudden discouragement about it all. He wonders whether it is worthwhile. Old doubts and feelings, which he thought were far behind him, suddenly loom up again. He is stabbed by dread that the whole thing may be only a dream world of his own illusions. Such periods of temptation are perfectly normal; expect them to come. Such a crisis came to George Fox, founder of the Society of Friends. He waited patiently. Suddenly, the dawn broke through with peaceful assurance.

Another crisis is the uneasiness of self-condemnation. There is no one in the entire world who condemns you. You yourself are the only person who condemns you — and pointlessly. In reality, there is no condemnation whatever, but, as long as you think there is, you ache. Not only that, but a man dwelling with the illusion of self-condemnation is compulsively driven to do things that increase the illusion. There is no man, nor god, nor past experience to condemn you. You are free and you are free right now. Will you try to see this?

Go all out to contact Higher Power. Do not take half measures. Do not hesitate to ask boldly for far more. Who asks a king for a penny?

## Abandon Human Effort

We remain weak as long as we cling to unhealthy attitudes. What if a man bought a prize-winner steer and fed it all sorts of delicacies that he assumed the steer would like, rather than what nature decrees? That steer would win no more prizes. Likewise, we must not set up stubborn assumptions about what we need. The test of a genuine need is so simple that millions miss it: Does it make me genuinely happy, or does it lead to even more despair?

Unhealthy attitudes lurk behind all personal tragedies. What an incredible situation! I have known hundreds of people living their lives on the rocks of alcoholism, emotionally-induced illness, sex frustrations. Do you know what they fear when I point out the need for dismissing their destructive attitudes? They fear that by giving them up they will lose control of their lives!

Receptivity to right ideas places us in the right position. If we want an elevator to carry us upward, we cannot stand in the street. We must stand upon the surface capable of uplifting us. We must stand with a mind courageously willing to abandon lower levels. By standing on the platform of Reality, it lifts us all by itself.

We should be very glad we get tired of working so hard at living. The abandonment of useless human effort is just the thing we need for contacting Higher Power. By abandonment I mean setting aside ego-directed drives, such as planning, contriving, desiring, hoping, yearning, speculating, demanding, straining, claiming, influencing, dominating. All these interfere with the natural flow of the inner life. We contact the Higher Power only as we loosen our attachments to them. And then, at some magic moment, we change from driven men to carried men.

No one should ever feel bad if Self-Observation reveals that he or she is presently on a lower level. On the contrary, we should be glad, for only this discovery makes upliftment possible. It is the foolish person who imagines he has nothing to learn. Also, remember, the Mystic Path has no moral judgments. There are no such things as good and bad, superior or inferior. We don't consider a five-year old child inferior to a child of ten. We simply realize that everyone is on a different level of insight and awareness.

As you cover all these ideas, let your previous studies in religion or psychology enter. You will see how everything agrees.

My own early search and study covered enough books to fill a small library. I investigated every teacher and system from Aristotle and Apolinarianism to Zeno and Zen. The teachings varied in outer forms, but all agreed on the essentials: Man's task is to awaken to his true identity. The Kingdom of Heaven is within. Spiritual truths are discovered with an entirely new kind of thinking, quite distinct and vastly superior to the mind that builds bridges and sells merchandise.

## Sure Steps to Awakening

Along the Mystic Path we, again and again, come across the sign: *Wake up!* In this section we meet a number of short and effective eye-openers:

People think that life has hundreds of problems. It hasn't. There is only one problem. The lost child doesn't know the way home.

*The Truth is stronger than thought, emotion, desire, sex, regret, money, fear, boredom, the past, the future; stronger than anything in life. None of these can ever trouble the mystic-man.*

When new students came to the Greek philosopher, Pythagoras, the very first lesson they heard was, "Learn to be silent. Let your quiet mind listen and absorb."

*We try to reassure ourselves with our human thoughts, but mental gymnastics cannot help us and we know it. Trying to uplift ourselves with conditioned ideas is like trying to get upstairs by pacing around the basement. A new kind of mind is needed.*

The less your external comforts from friends, position, money, the more your inner comfort from the Higher Power. Now, whatever you do, do not take this as religious or philosophical speculation. Take it as a practical fact, for that is exactly what it is.

*A perfect method for awakening is to examine the results of our daily actions. If they are harmful, we know we need more consciousness.*

The reason Truth affects a man so powerfully is because he already knows it deep within. All emotional feeling toward Truth is a response, a recognition. We may accept it, or reject it, but we see it.

*We cannot be free of nagging desires through suppression. That is like trying to keep a rubber boat beneath the water. But we can remove compulsive desires altogether by understanding their nature.*

Whenever you work in harmony with a mystic principle, you ally yourself with a force ten-thousand times greater than you know.

*Awakening starts when we actually see our hypnosis. We must suspect that we are entirely different people than we thought we were.*

You can be guided accurately by an inner voice, but your first task is to separate it from all the counterfeits. And someday you will see that this inner sense of guidance was right all along.

*Since distress is caused and felt by the artificial self, ask, "If I extinguish this false self, who is left to get distressed?" There is no one left.*

The Mystic Path has the simplest morality possible: Whatever helps us to awaken is right; whatever keeps us hypnotized is wrong.

## Fifteen Ways to Gain New Strength

Fresh energy flows from you into every daily project when you:

1. See the attractiveness of the higher life.

2. *Don't accept unhappiness as necessary.*

3. Increase your self-awareness.

4. *Abandon self-defeating attitudes.*

5. Insist upon strict self-honesty.

6. *Try to understand your desires.*

7. Make simple and persistent efforts.

8. *Refuse to sacrifice your integrity to anyone.*

9. No longer take excitement as happiness.

10. *Stop wasting energy in negative emotions.*

11. Make self-change your aim in life.

12. *Don't identify with anything.*

13. Listen carefully to mystical principles.

14. *Make self-discovery your daily hobby.*

15. Want the Truth more than anything else.

Select any one of these as your mental exercise for the next few days. Think it through, try to see its full significance.

That is how you add new strength.

Let's illustrate point 1: *See the attractiveness of the higher life:*

A young archer was imprisoned for accidentally trespassing upon the king's private hunting grounds. The king, notorious for his harsh justice, ordered the young man imprisoned indefinitely. Though allowed to roam around the prison yard, he could see nothing of the outside world, for the prison was surrounded by a tall wall of eucalyptus trees. Years passed. The prisoner gradually lost interest in the outside world. He felt a dull sort of comfort in his routine existence. He walked about as if in a daze, performing his labors mechanically. To most of his guards he appeared content, but one or two noticed a horrifying hostility deep down in his eyes.

One day a new and kindly king took the throne. Hearing of the prisoner, he ordered his release. His jailers took him to the prison gate and opened it wide. The prisoner glanced puzzledly and apprehensively outward, then turned around and walked back to his cell.

The king, as wise as he was kindly, gave new instructions: "Each morning set a new attraction outside the gate. Set them progressively farther and farther away. Then, open the gate before the prisoner."

The attractions were set out as instructed. One morning the attraction was a friendly villager, then new clothing, then fresh fruits.

Step by step, the prisoner lost his liking for the habitual and suppressed life. Each new attraction of the other world gave him a fresh sense of freedom. Gradually, he led himself to liberty and happiness.

Anyone who feels imprisoned by life can do likewise.

## Freedom from Injustice

Baffled by what happens to you? You cannot see why this defeat or that sorrow comes your way? These perplexities are daily events to millions of people.

The mystic-man knows why things happen as they do. Better yet, he knows the solution — his own awakened state.

We can take a common complaint and see both its cause and solution — the *only* solution you will ever find:

"With all our laws and moral persuasions, why is there so much injustice in the world?"

"Because hypnotized men are incapable of justice. I must speak very frankly to you about this. Please follow very carefully."

"We'll follow."

"A hypnotized man's only idea of justice is having what he wants, what he insists he has coming to him. If he gets his demand, to him that is justice. If denied, he calls it injustice. His entire false scale of justice rests on whether or not he gets his demand. This is why we have endless conflict between people and nations. No one ever stops to inquire whether his very demands may be unhealthy or unnecessary to his true interests."

"Then there can be no justice among hypnotized men? How dreadful."

"Not dreadful for *you*, if *you* are awake. Again, please follow carefully; you have no idea of the gold here. When you are awake, human injustice cannot possibly hurt you. No matter *what* happens, you are at peace."

"I don't understand how this is possible."

"The government taxes you unjustly? You are not your money; you cannot lose *yourself*. Your spouse betrays you? You have not abandoned your true individuality to him or her, so you retain your inner quietness."

"If only I could believe that!"

"Don't try. Persist along the Mystic Path. You will have the personal experience of all this. You can live among every sort of human injustice and it will be as nothing to you. I am not speaking religiously or idealistically. I am giving you a fact."

"Yes, I sense that you know what you are talking about. It is just that I'm not awake enough to comprehend."

"Let the habitual human self fade away. Seek to contact the Higher Power. You'll be amazed at how feelings of injustice fade away as far as *you* are concerned. Nobody and nothing can touch you. How can a runaway car hurt someone soaring high in an airplane?"

## Overcoming Barriers to Higher Power

What prevents our contact with the force above human mind-power? It is essential to know and to end it.

Simply stated, it is negativity; *all* forms of negativity. Like a block of wood prevents two magnets from drawing together, so does negativity block us from our good.

Recall this mystic principle: We must become aware of a negativity before it can be destroyed. It is absolutely impossible to break free from a harmful state as long as we are not conscious of its existence. It is highly heroic to suspect that we might have unseen negativities.

Shocks and crises reveal them. A person meeting business failure, ill health, disgrace, or rejection has a wonderful opportunity to observe negative reactions. How amazing! The very shock we dislike so intensely is trying to tell us something of extraordinary value. The false self, the cause of all our troubles, is self-destructive. Having shocked us, we can use the shock to destroy the false self. This is what the wise mystic does.

One reason we cling to negative states is that they give us a strange sort of pleasure. For instance, a person rejecting a helpful truth can pretend that he is a strong and independent thinker who needs nothing from anyone. We must ask whether we are willing to give up such unhealthy feelings in order to find healthy pleasure in psychic maturity.

Remember, it is taking a positive action to remove the negative. Is it good or bad to remove weeds from a garden?

We have been fooled long enough. We must make up our minds on that point. You have paid enough; it is time to quit. Quit thinking that you must halt before the barrier of inner negativity. You need not. You can crash through. There is not a single harmful thought, or emotion, or circumstance that can really separate you from the lofty life. Wherever we see a negative state, that is where we can destroy it.

"All these things you say arouse strong reactions in me. I can't explain them, but they are quite different from my usual feelings. Why do I react like this?"

"Because there is something in you that *knows*."

## *To contact higher power*

1. You presently possess a Force entirely different from human mind-power and vastly superior to it.

2. Use your mind to raise the sails, but let the winds of psychic awareness carry you forward.

3. Human thought-power is useful and necessary for human affairs. Spiritual awareness is necessary for inner freedom.

4. You will win!

5. Take orders only from the headquarters of your True Self.

6. There is no condemnation whatsoever. This becomes a relieving fact when you really see it.

7. If it helps us to awaken, it is right. If it keeps us asleep, it is wrong.

8. Nothing, absolutely nothing, is more attractive than the New Life existing outside the walls of the ego-self.

9. You can so transform yourself that you will never again be pained by feelings of injustice.

10. As we remove negativity, contact with Higher Power grows stronger.

# 6

# The Power
# of Love
# Among People

We have seen that everything in our day can be used for self-enrichment. In this chapter we will discover the mystical way to healthy human relations which lead to that supreme state called love. These principles present you with entirely new ways for living in self-harmony while living with others.

Ask fifty people for their definition of love and you receive fifty different answers. Obviously, love is not something that the conditioned human mind can discover through personal viewpoints. Human reasoning can have opinions and attitudes about love, but only a spiritually attuned mind can *know*.

The mystics have a practical system for getting at the truth about anything, including love. It can be termed the "Not this and not that" method. By systematically discarding everything that love is *not,* we finally arrive at what it *is* — just as gold is left after clearing the pebbles.

Love is not dependency, idolization, sentimentality, craving, or physical attraction. Human relationships based on these attributes are strained, ready to break apart at any moment.

Genuine love does not start with an emotion. It begins with a state of consciousness, of clear awareness, of a deep understanding of both the self and the other person. Then, the emotions arising from this are legitimate, natural fruit. Tenderness and affection are among them. When an emotion comes first, it is not genuine love, only a counterfeit, which is really craving, or passion, or a wish to flee from an unwanted self into the other person.

Mystical love cannot be based on desire or craving. People sometimes say, "I have a painful craving for a certain person of the opposite sex whom I cannot have. How can I relieve my mind of this torture?"

"Try to see that the craving is not based on actual qualities of the other person, but rather in your idealistic imagination of him. He represents something you need, perhaps strength, or security, or affection. But this ideal is merely a *need in you* which you mistakenly assume is a *reality in him.* Try to see this. As you succeed, you will be astonished at how differently you see this so-called ideal person. He or she has not changed; *you* have."

## The Maiden at the Stream

A remarkable feature of mystical love is that it is both deeply personal, yet unattached. To unknowing people it often appears cold and blunt. But beneath the surface, it is warm, caring, responsive. It is the nature of authentic love to ignore the external impressions it makes on others, favorable or unfavorable. It does not care what people think; it does what its very compassionate nature impels it to do. Exterior show belongs to pseudo-love, motivated by

89

self-glory in hope of attracting public praise.

The story is told of two disciples of mysticism who were returning one afternoon to their monastery. They came to a bridgeless stream where a pretty maiden sought to cross. When the first disciple announced his intention of carrying her across, his shocked companion objected, "No! We are sworn to purity. It violates our vows to even touch a woman." Ignoring the objection, the first disciple boldly picked the woman up, waded across the stream, set her down and went on his way. For the next several miles, he was indignantly accused of conduct unbecoming a disciple. Finally, the first man turned to his companion and remarked, "Look. I left that woman back at the stream — you are still carrying her."

Love is like that. It does what it sees to do and lets it go at that. "Perfect kindness acts without thinking of kindness." (Lao-tse)

Love is a state of psychic understanding. Lack of love is lack of comprehension. What must we understand? Take fear. The New Testament states that perfect love casts out fear. Fear arises in human relations whenever we want something from someone and worry that we won't get it. The mystic-man has no fear because he has no demands upon others; he lives bountifully from his Kingdom of Heaven within. A love relationship is impossible when based on demand, subtle or obvious. Such pseudo-love is merely a bargain: "You be nice to me and I'll be nice to you, but, if you cease to please me, I'll go away." The mystic life has none of that. It is an entirely different world.

## The Mystic's Compassion

How does the mystic see humanity? In an entirely different way from ordinary men and women. It is profitable for us also to see people from a mystical viewpoint. It provides power.

The enlightened mystic sees human beings as little

children. The children are sometimes nice and sometimes not so nice. If they behave badly, he knows it is because they have not as yet made contact with their spiritual being within.

He sees them as secret sufferers, for that is always the condition of little children in spiritual darkness. He has great compassion toward them, knowing the price they must continue to pay until they use their very suffering as a liberating teacher. He is like a father who hears his child call out in distress when they are separated in a crowd. While knowing that the distress is genuine, he also knows that the child need only look in the right direction to make everything all right.

"You are loved," the mystic never ceases to proclaim, "far more than you think."

Where ordinary man habitually blames and accuses others, the mystic has none of it. He knows why people behave as they do; he has no illusions that people could behave better if only their circumstances were different. He knows that wickedness is performed mechanically, unconsciously, by hypnotized people who think they are awake. Do you, he asks, *blame* an automobile for loosening its brakes and crashing into a building? No, you understand that an automobile does not know what it does to itself and to others.

But make no mistake, the mystic is not soft. He coddles no one. He is the toughest teacher on earth. Love won't permit him to let others get away with it. The truth must be told at all costs, no matter who it hurts or how much. While not blaming a human machine for running wild, he insists that it cease to be a machine and turn into its birthright as a conscious human being.

George Gurdjieff once remarked that true love consists in aiding another's development all the while knowing full well that the other person may snap at the extended helping hand. The loving person must willingly take the hostility of those he tries to help, just as a ranger takes the snarls of a bear with a thorn in its foot.

The spiritual man's compassion springs from his insight into things as they are. Not only does he know that a New World exists but he dwells in it.

How utterly satisfying it is to know that, in spite of all appearances in the familiar world, nevertheless when *this* light shines it is all seen to be good — unutterably good. In the dimness of our normal state of consciousness we see strife and struggle, suffering and injustice, evil and torture, anguish and failure. But when the veils are withdrawn in a moment of insight, the mystics, with no dissentient voice, speak of the omnipresent overflowing Joy at the heart of things, of "unbounded glorious Love." [1]

## Twenty Special Secrets

1. When two people meet, the prize always goes to the one with the most self-insight. He will be calmer, more confident, more at ease with the other.
2. *Never permit the behavior of other people to tell you how to feel.*
3. Pay little attention to what people say or do. Instead, try to see their innermost motive for speaking and acting. (Now, apply this very same rule to yourself and you become an enlightened person!)
4. *Any friendship requiring the submission of your original nature and dignity to another person is all wrong.*
5. Mystically speaking, there is no difference between you and another person. This is why we cannot hurt another without hurting ourselves, nor help another without helping ourselves.
6. *When we are free of all unnecessary desires toward other people, we can never be deceived or hurt.*

[1] Raynor C. Johnson, *The Imprisoned Splendour* (New York: Harper & Row, Publishers, Inc., 1953).

7. You take a giant step toward psychological maturity when you refuse to angrily defend yourself against unjust slander. For one thing, resistance disturbs your own peace of mind.

8. *You understand others to the exact degree that you really understand yourself. Work for more self-knowledge.*

9. Do not be afraid to fully experience everything that happens to you in your human relations, especially the pains and disappointments. Do this and every thing becomes clear at last.

10. *The individual who really knows what it means to love has no anxiety when his love is unseen or rejected.*

11. If you painfully lose a valuable friend, do not rush out at once for a replacement. Such action prevents you from examining your heartache and breaking free of it.

12. *Do not be afraid to be a nobody in the social world. This is a deeper and richer truth than appears on the surface.*

13. Every unpleasant experience with another person is an opportunity to see people as they are, not as we mistakenly idealize them. The more unpleasant the other person is, the more he can teach you.

14. *You can be so wonderfully free from a sense of injury and injustice that you are surprised when you hear others complain of them.*

15. We cannot recognize a virtue in another person that we do not possess in ourselves. It takes a truly loving and patient person to recognize those virtues in another.

16. *Do not mistake desire for love. Desire leaves home in a frantic search for one gratification after another. Love is at home with itself.*

17. There are parts of you that want the loving life and

parts that do not. Place yourself on the side of your positive forces; do all you can to aid and encourage them.

18. *You must stop living so timidly, from fixed fears of what others will think of you and of what you will think of yourself.*

19. Do not contrive to be a loving person; work to be a real person. Being real is being loving.

20. *The greatest love you could ever offer to another is to so transform your inner life that others are attracted to your genuine example of goodness.*

## Answers to Questions About Love

"I know I behave unlovingly at times. How can I break the pattern?"

"Whenever it happens, do not agree with it internally. Supreme Knowledge within each of us speaks reproval whenever we act without love. Listen to that voice, not to your harsh behavior. A person can go on for months or years under the hypnosis of the unkindly false self, but by constantly disagreeing with it, the pattern changes. Observe your unkind behavior. Refuse to accept it as your real self. Gradually, you bring exterior action into line with the loving interior, just as a good father influences his unruly son for good."

"Why is it so shocking to lose someone we love?"

"Because it brings us face to face with our own emptiness. If the marriage falls apart, or the sweetheart goes away, the sufferer's first urge is to find a replacement to fill the void. You do this because you are scared, insecure, you feel unwanted and unloved. But, even if you find a replacement, it does nothing for you, not really. The trembling is still there, only covered up. If a break-up occurs, examine your own driving need to find security in a replacement. Insight reveals that it can do nothing for you. Then, beyond that shocking fact you make an amazing discovery: You see that the only security is in the truth itself. From that point on, all your relations with the opposite sex are entirely different. Because there is no fear, there is genuine love."

"How can I get people to act as I wish?"

"You must have no ideas whatever as to how people should behave toward you. You want them to turn left. They turn right. You hope they do this. They do that. Why do you get hurt? Not because of what people do but because you have demanded they should do as you wish. Abolish all demands; then, people can behave any way they like while you remain at peace."

"What happens when a self-aware person meets one still in psychic slumber? I mean, is it possible for them to love each other, for instance, when man meets woman?"

"A self-aware person can love a non-aware person, but the reverse is impossible. Two conscious human beings can exchange love, but two unawakened people cannot. How can they exchange a love they don't have? Love comes with awakening. Hypnotized people can only give what they *call* love, for example, mutual flattery. Their relationship is based on desire, not love. This is easily observed. Notice how quickly the so-called love turns to resentment when a particular desire is denied or thwarted."

## How to Develop Love-Capacity

"Why all this contradiction in people? We talk so much about love but behave just the opposite."

"Most talk about love is just that — talk. A man must behave according to his level of psychic development. No one can possibly behave on a higher level of love than the level he actually occupies. But remember, human beings are very cunning with exterior *appearances* of love, so don't be fooled. By self-work, a man can raise his love-level. Then, he will behave differently, with more genuine compassion. That is an objective of the Mystic Path. We want to uplift our compassion by raising our spiritual level."

"You once said that we develop our love-capacity by patiently enduring unloving words and actions from others. How?"

"Be willing to give up immediate and unhealthy pleasures for long-term riches. You may get an immediate sensation of pleasure by snapping back at an unkind person, but, if you do, you have lost a great opportunity for advancing your inner self. Instead, discover why you needed to snap back. You will discover your action sprang from the touchy ego-self. That very observation in itself weakens the ego."

"I used to think that my whirlpool of social activities sprang from my love of people, from wanting to help them and to be with them. But now I feel oppressed by all these maddening involvements and wonder why I continue."

"You do them not because they mean anything to you but because they distract you from your inner blankness. You just don't know what else to do with yourself. Pull out. Do it gradually if you like, but, for your mental and spiritual health, pull out. Get off by yourself and ask yourself whether you really want this kind of life. Honest inquiry will produce a tremendous sigh of relief. Now, you are starting to enjoy your life, for you are no longer sacrificing it to frantic involvements."

"Why are human relations so painful? What can we do to ease the stress and anxiety?"

"In previous discussions, we saw that suffering is destroyed by bringing it up from the unconscious to the conscious level. Connect this with your human relations. Try to see how much pain you have because of unconscious hopes, demands, expectations, fears, and desires toward others. You want them to act in a way that pleases you. You desire friendship, conversation, sex, and so on. Try to see — really work at it — try to see that these very desires cause your pain, for you fear their failure. Now, can you abandon them? If so, suffering is impossible. You experience a fantastic relief, just like breaking through an entangling net."

## The Power of Psychic Awakening

Every man does the best he knows how, but no one actually does his best. Socrates points out that man's basic error lies in ignorance of his true nature. This ignorance leads to false and fleeting values. Spiritual awakening corrects his values so that he cheerfully cherishes wisdom, and gentleness, and old-fashioned goodness.

As we awaken from psychic sleep, we see others in a new way. They look entirely different from before. We may think that they have changed, when, really, it is ourselves who have altered. This introduces many rich benefits. For one thing, we can clearly distinguish between people on a higher level of understanding and those on a lower level. This is the same as seeing that people occupy different levels of love, for understanding *is* love. This insight leads us to seek out those on the higher level, for they are the ones with whom we now have more in common. There is no sense of superiority in leaving former friends; we just realize that we must go upward. With them or without them, we must go on.

Another healthy benefit derived is that of no longer fearing resentment, or disapproval, or accusation from others. You clearly see that *their negative attacks belong to them; they have nothing whatsoever to do with you.* Do *you* feel ill just because someone else does? It is like that.

Psychic awakening creates smooth relations with understanding. Strong people understand weak people. The unpleasant or disloyal behavior of weak people cannot distress those who are genuinely strong. But unawakened people cannot live together harmoniously. They see and dislike weaknesses in others that unconsciously they have and dislike in themselves. This causes irritation, impatience, all sorts of grief. The only cure is spiritual strength. The only strength is Truth.

Sooner or later, along the Mystic Path, we make an enlightening discovery. We see that we cannot behave unlovingly toward others without paying the price in psychic disturbance. "Does anyone do wrong? It is to himself that he does the wrong." (Marcus Aurelius) At one time we may have thought this was a moralistic platitude just fine to teach children, but not applicable to a harsh world. Now we know it to be an unbreakable law of life. We see that unkind behavior is like burning down our homes in order to strike back at unpleasant guests. But, at the same time, we also see the positive side of the law: We cannot love another without doing good to ourselves.

The above ideas are typical of those explored in Mystic Path Study Groups. The dominating purpose of a Mystic Path Study Group is to understand and to pass on this resounding message:

"In all the wide world there is only one place where we can truly get away from it all. That place is the psychic vacationland within ourselves."

## How to Handle Difficulties with People

From the mystical viewpoint there is no such thing as difficulties with other people; the only difficulty is within ourselves. We need only to clear our own psychological confusions; then, that inner clarity enables us to handle anything coming from the outside. On the human level we may find others to be troublesome and disloyal, but, if our essential self dwells on the spiritual level, we cannot be injured. Like this:

"I suppose I'm too sensitive, but how can I prevent people from hurting my feelings?"

"No one on earth can hurt you, unless you accept the hurt in your own mind. What if you are offered a sour apple but refuse to take it? To whom does the sourness belong? As the false sense of self falls away, so does your acceptance of the sour apples of criticism and unkindness from others. The problem is not other people; it is your reaction."

Let's see how increased insight changes our attitudes and, thereby, lessens our difficulties with others. Our awakened awareness reveals that nobody is really as happy as we previously thought. We see through the masks that people wear; we see how hard they work to convince themselves and others that all is well. It's all an act, and how clearly we realize it. Their nervous social and business pursuits, and their empty amusements, no longer fool us. We know they wake up the next morning with dread of the day.

We understand all this because we have first seen through our own pretenses. They are repeating the very same wearisome stage performance that used to keep us so tired.

This completely alters our viewpoints and relations. We are no longer critical or envious. Our previous envy sprang from the illusion that others had more out of life than we, but now we know better. We see them as secret sufferers, just as we used to be. Seeing this, we can no longer think or act harshly toward them. Henry Wadsworth Longfellow once remarked that if we could see the concealed sorrows of others, we would be very tender toward them.

We forgive them as we forgave ourselves. Our new gentleness toward ourselves can now extend itself freely to others.

And now we understand something for the first time, something previously blocked by pride and vanity: Love is not of the human self, but of the Supreme within us. This makes us smile for a dozen reasons; one, being that we need no longer work at love; we need only rest in the Supreme, which is love itself.

From this lofty height, various expressions of love among people, including affection, drift down.

A world of weary people yearns for affection. What a sadly needed form of love is affection, whether it be a cheery word, or an understanding nod, or a touch of the hand. Rich people would gladly give up their treasures for this precious jewel. Those with power and prestige would exchange everything for someone with whom they could experience the affectionate way of life.

Exchange of affection between two people, perhaps man and woman, is possible only when both possess the capacity. It cannot be one-sided. A person capable of giving genuine affection will also be able to receive it, for they are two parts of the single ability, just as a wave advances and recedes.

Affection grows naturally as we awaken to our true nature.

## An Esoteric Revelation About Love

Lasting love infills the individual living from his True Self. The True Self *is* love. It is impossible for people living from their authentic identities to quarrel or hurt each other. They do not and cannot see another person as a rival, or as a threat. The other person is not a separate identity to be feared; therefore, only quiet understanding passes back and forth between them. There is no impulsive behavior or thoughtless mistakes. "Love is infallible; it has no errors, for all errors are the want of love." (William Law)

We may see each other as being individual in physical appearance and as being different in human personality, but we do not see others as being different in spiritual identity. We are One. Just as the moon reflects the same light in several ponds, so are we the individual reflections of the Single Supreme.

Any effort of the false self toward love is unnatural in

100

appearance and tragic in consequence. Lebanese poet and mystic, Kahlil Gibran, once declared that men and women lose the spirit of love because of their own wrong concepts about it. Love is not what the conditioned human mind *wants* it to be, but always what it *really* is. A false desire for love to be this or that is like adding paint to a river in order to give color to a waterfall. Love must be left alone by the mind; it must be permitted to be exactly what it is. Love, when left alone, glows in all its natural beauty.

Problems relating to love will never again cause distress, once you grasp this esoteric secret: Love does not arise from the conditioned human mind. Thinking about love is not the same as knowing love. The mind must break through its social conditioning and enter an awareness of Reality, which is love. Then, we rest from concern over all things, including the need to have someone to love and someone to love us. Referring to Christ's teaching to take no thought for tomorrow, Dr. Paul Brunton explains:

> He meant that we should cease worrying, cease being anxious, let go of all disturbing thoughts, and resign all problems to the Overself, to the higher power. By logical, rational thinking, you may find a human solution, but by ceasing to think, by taking no thought and relinquishing your problem, the higher power is then given an opportunity to deal with it. To take no thought means to still the mind; to sit and enter into real meditation. Thereby the Overself is given a chance to come and take thought on your behalf for you.[2]

We must be like Jason who was promised the Golden Fleece, if he would perform certain heroic tasks. In spite of all his suspense and uncertainty, he boldly accepted the challenge. One by one, he achieved the seemingly impossible, aided by the magic skill of the princess Medea.

So can we accept the challenges of the Mystic Path,

---

[2] Paul Brunton, *Discover Yourself* (New York: E. P. Dutton & Co., Inc., 1939).

regardless of our deep doubts and confusions. And so can we, aided by the magical Higher Power, turn impossibilities into living victories.

## *Truths in this chapter about the power of love*

1. You can use every human relationship to build a life of love.
2. We discern love's authentic nature by first seeing what it is not.
3. Love is a state of psychic understanding, of elevated awareness.
4. You are loved far more than you think.
5. To be considerate of others without their knowledge is love in action.
6. To be real is to be loving.
7. Our love-capacity develops spontaneously as we sincerely walk the Mystic Path.
8. Self-understanding leads to other-understanding which leads to compassion and gentleness.
9. Love is not of the conditioned mind, but of the Supreme.
10. When we are fully loving we have no cares whatsoever.

# 7

# How to Stop Heartache and Suffering

If we want to end a disturbing condition in our business affairs, we study that condition. If we wish to correct a mistake in directions while traveling on vacation, we study a map. That is exactly what we must do with heartache and suffering. We must study them just as carefully as any other condition we wish to correct.

We don't want temporary relief. We want to end it once and for all. Mere relief is like taking aspirin every day for a headache. Why not destroy the very cause of the headache once and for all so that daily relief is unnecessary? It can be done.

Start with this:

Whenever you suffer from anything whatsoever, remember that it could have been avoided. Simply remember that had you understood the Mystic Path more fully, you would not have felt that pain. This helps you to work with yourself today, so that tomorrow will be serene.

What, exactly, is suffering?

Our pains are caused by our wrong viewpoints toward things. The false self throws up an imaginary picture of how it insists things *should* be. And every time this *should* be clashes with what *actually happens*, we react painfully. The problem is not what actually happens, but our demands that something else should happen. Don't take my word for this; experiment for yourself.

Of course, human beings don't like it when advised to give up illusory demands for this or that. It saddens us. Living in illusions gives one a false sense of aliveness, so we fear to be without them. It is like feeling sad when the doctor advises us to give up tainted food!

To repeat, pain appears whenever a desire for a particular happening clashes with what actually happens. We want someone to appreciate us. When he doesn't, we are sad. We hope for the office promotion. Someone else gets it and we fall into gloom. We hope to keep a friend. He goes away, leaving us with heartache.

The pain may be major or minor, noticeable or subconscious, but it always swells up whenever a desire smashes against the wall of reality. This fact alone should prompt the serious seeker to thoroughly investigate his desires and yearnings.

## A Vital Secret for You

So how does pain cease? Not by avoiding involvement with life, for this merely sets up a hard wall of resistance, which causes fear. And not by building up lots of friendships so that if one fails we have another. This is an attempt to find security by attachment to others, which only creates more insecurity. "There is no consolation except in truth alone." (Blaise Pascal)

So how? The entire book answers this, but we will

105

explore several specific answers.

"May we pause here for a question? You say that suffering is an illusion, but it feels quite real to *me*."

"Suffering is *caused* by an illusion. By living from the illusory false self, we encounter pain. But when awareness of the truth dissolves the false self, who is there left to suffer? How can a nonexistent person suffer? Try to grasp this; it is so important to you. To repeat a previous example, suppose some night you have a dreadful nightmare. It tortures you. But when you wake up and see it as a nightmare, do you still suffer? What person is there to suffer? None."

Dr. Hubert Benoit presents the clearest explanation of this that I have ever found:

> Anguish is then an illusion since its causes are illusory. Besides this theoretical demonstration we can obtain a practical demonstration of it: we can prove directly, intuitively, the illusory character of anguish. If in fact at a moment at which I suffer ... I shift my attention from my thinking to my feeling, if, leaving aside all my mental images, I apply myself to perceiving in myself the famous moral suffering in order to savour it and to find out at last what it is — I do not succeed ... of suffering itself I do not find a scrap. The more I pay attention to the act of feeling, withdrawing thereby my attention from my imaginative film, the less I feel. And I prove then the unreality of anguish.[1]

Say, for example, the mind runs an imaginative film about some foolishness in our past. That stream of thought causes painful guilt and shame. So we suffer anguish. But the feeling is false, because it is based on mere thought about something that is not *now* happening and which has nothing to do with us right now. But by permitting the imaginative film, we also permit the illusion that it is happening now, which causes pain.

---

[1] From *The Supreme Doctrine* by Hubert Benoit. © Copyright 1955 by Pantheon Books, Inc. Reprinted by permission of Random House, Inc.

## How Pain Magically Disappears

Let's see how we can call the bluff of these negative films: Suppose an anonymous voice on the telephone tells you that a tiger is prowling in the basement of your house. You scoff, hang up, go about your business. But you sense a strange uneasiness. Your imagination runs a film of a tiger prowling the basement. Realizing that what bothers you is the imagination, you turn on the basement light and look down. No tiger. You are relieved. Your anguish vanishes. You wonder why you did not look down immediately when you felt the anxiety.

That is exactly what happens in the psychological world. The mind unreels an imaginative film which frightens us. Then, we mistakenly assume that the fright is based on reality, which it is not. The tiger is not really there. We have the relief of that fact when we simply *see* that fact.

Marcus Aurelius comes to the point: "Erase the imagination."

If we awaken ourselves long enough to erase the imaginative film and to search for the pain caused by it, what happens? Magic! The pain cannot be found. Why? Just as the awakening sun dissolves fog, so does our conscious awareness of pain make it disappear. Try it. Keep trying. It makes magic.

A collie and a wolf found themselves traveling together along the coast. Coming to a bay, they decided to save time by paddling across on a log.

"By the way," the wolf boastfully declared as they paddled along, "I am considered an authority on the science of the sea. Suppose we pass time by discussing the tides and currents."

"Sorry," replied the collie, "but when it comes to the sea I know only one thing."

"Well, then," the wolf spoke up, "I am also famous around the forest for my seagoing philosophies. Suppose we meditate together upon the ocean's beauty and grandeur."

"I am afraid," the collie told his companion, "that regarding the ocean I know only one thing."

At that moment a sudden wave washed both travelers into the water. The wolf splashed helplessly about, calling for help. The collie skillfully towed him back to shore.

"Too bad," the collie explained to the gasping wolf, "that we couldn't discuss science and philosophy out there, but, when it comes to the ocean, I know only one thing — how to swim."

There we have the very heart of the Mystic Path. Never mind discussions, or philosophies, or fancy phrases. When it comes to heartache, or any other problem in life, we need do just one thing—*learn how to swim.*

## Don't Make This Mistake

See how all this connects with the basic technique of impartial Self-Observation. Witness the passage of mental and emotional grief. Watch it pass through you. Do not resist what you see. Do not identify with it, that is, do not take the painful feeling as being part of the essential you. *You* are someone entirely different. Separate the pain from the person you call "I". This is a challenging practice at first, but it produces amazing results. You have here a mystical technique that changes your life. I assure you of this.

It is as though a man had a pocketful of firecrackers that exploded one after another. If he fails to see that they are within his own system, he cannot get rid of them. But if he holds them at arm's length for examination, the very examination tells him to toss them away.

"I don't understand the need for bringing our pains up to the surface of conscious awareness. Why not keep them hidden away so that they won't bother us?"

"That is a serious mistake made by millions. Repressed negativities cause inner turmoil, whether you are aware of them or not. A hurricane in the darkness of the night is just as destructive as during the day."

"You are saying that whatever we refuse to face consciously, we must suffer from unconsciously."

"Right. And don't take it as a psychological assumption; take it as the fact it is. Let me show you a small but typical pain that is experienced by many people without their slightest awareness. It has to do with the painful feeling that one has missed out on opportunities in life. A man reads in the newspaper that a certain piece of property in his neighborhood that had been worth ten thousand dollars five years ago is now worth twenty thousand dollars. The man feels a poke of pain. He kicks himself for not buying the property; he feels like a fool, a failure."

"You are describing me!"

"You can be entirely free from such pokes of pain. It won't make any difference to you whether you bought the property or not. But you must start by seeing that the pangs are actually within you. You cannot escape prison if you insist you are not in one."

We must see that our negative emotions are self-induced suffering, for that is exactly what they are. Can we be angry and happy at the same time? Of course not. Can we be in a mood of depression and enjoy ourselves? No. Is it possible to be on fire with worry and still have a pleasant day? Obviously not. Here is a great clue: See all negative feelings as pointless pain. That will aid you to understand and to remove them.

By the way, all this is not a grim task. It is really a lot of fun.

## The Hunter

So runs my dream; but what am I?
An infant crying in the night:
An infant crying for the light:
And with no language but a cry.

— Alfred Tennyson

Tears can stop trickling. That is why we are walking the Mystic Path. It shows us how.

Let me introduce you to a personal term of mine I call a Higher Hint. A Higher Hint comes to the person who has reached the end of his ego-endurance. He catches a Higher Hint, a vague and mysterious feeling that he can no longer use his human logic and reasoning to save himself. He dimly recognizes the inadequacy of his present self-structure. His mental supports are collapsing beneath him.

Such a man is awakening to the light! Having abandoned the false — with fear and trembling — he catches his first Higher Hint of the true. He is face to face with the greatest secret on earth — the New Life.

A hunter, stalking game in the jungle, fell into a deep well, abandoned long ago by the natives. The bottom of the well was shallowly covered with water from an underground stream that entered and exited from opposite crevices. Floundering around in the dim light, the hunter searched desperately around for a way out. To his delight he discovered several vines hanging down from the walls of the well. Grabbing one, he struggled upward, but, a moment later, the vine snapped apart, spilling him into the water. He tried one vine after another, but all failed.

He stared fearfully at the single vine remaining. Should he try it or not? He realized the wave of horror that would sweep through him if he tried it and failed. Maybe, he reflected, he should wait awhile, comforting himself with the thought that the vine could rescue him any time he really wanted.

No, that was all wrong. Better to face the fact, one way or the other. With trembling hands he reached out, tugged on the vine. It tumbled down at his feet.

Utter despair.

Then, a strange thing happened. With the loss of hope, he sensed an entirely new kind of resourcefulness. It was something different, stronger, higher than anything he had known before.

Then he became aware of the water at his feet. It sparked an idea. Taking some heavy mud, he plugged the crevice where the water exited. As the well filled with water, he rose with it to the top.

Our Higher Hint comes when we have courage to face and abandon our false hopes. Then, we know exactly what to do. Then, effortlessly, we rise to the top of life.

## Lights Along The Mystic Path

People say to me, "But I *am* trying to liberate myself, yet nothing happens. In spite of all my efforts I remain as I am. Why?"

If you have ever asked this question, do not be concerned. It merely means that the seeker is still trying to grasp higher truths with the lower mind. It cannot be done. That is like trying to hear music by reading the printed notes. A new sense is needed, that of *awareness*. The everyday mind can lead to the door of the higher world but it cannot enter. This is of utmost importance to understand; it saves so much frustration. Notice how often the New Testament states that the human mind cannot comprehend cosmic concepts.

Awareness that we are not getting anywhere — listen to this! — awareness that we are not making progress *is actual progress*. It means that we have at last seen through our pretensions of progress, making way for the real thing.

Do not complicate your definition of awareness. We just need to know more about ourselves. That is all. We just need to learn more. And anyone can do that.

Take distress arising from mistakes. Making mistakes is just a lack of conscious knowledge of ourselves. Consciousness is light. Imagine yourself working around your home in total darkness, with the lights out of order. You stumble into furniture, use pepper instead of salt, perform awkward and even dangerous actions. But, as the

111

day dawns, you see better and act better. Finally, as the sun shines bright, so do all your actions. The more light of consciousness that is in your day, the smoother your work, the quieter your rest, the sunnier your smile.

Here are some lights along the way:

1. Nothing is too difficult for you to accomplish.
2. *The Truth teaches us what nothing else on earth can teach.*
3. Forget everything but self-advancement.
4. *The Truth will not start the walk for you, but it will match every step you take toward it with a step of its own toward you.*
5. If we have not enjoyed the last hour, we have wasted it.
6. *There is another Mind that thinks for you.*
7. Higher awareness is a lofty state, where you see amazing sights you never saw before.
8. *Suffering is not an enemy, but a guide to correction, like a temperature gauge in a hot room.*
9. Don't work so hard at living your life; just let it be lived.
10. *Like turning the wheel of your car in the right direction, a single wise turn of thought gives your life new direction.*

## The Value of a Crisis to You

Advancement to higher understanding is always preceded by a crisis of some kind. The greater the crisis the greater the opportunity for self-uplifting. Let's take an example: Suppose a man pretends that he really likes and enjoys other people. He acts out his pseudo-fondness by performing various acts of kindness that are commonly accepted as stemming from a kindly individual.

But this man is on the Mystic Path. This requires a strictly self-honest observation of how he *really* feels toward others. He shockingly finds that he really doesn't like other people at all. He is envious, competitive, resentful. He now sees that his exterior acts of kindness were only stage performances for public display. His *real* motive was to impress people, to persuade them to like him. Also, he behaved kindly in order to persuade *himself* that he was kindly.

He faces a severe crisis. Why? Because now he has his choice of honestly facing his self-deception, or of covering it up with rationalizations or excuses, or by simply refusing to look at it. If courageous, if wanting the truth above all, he will *enter* the crisis, that is, he will observe — as painful as it is for the time — his actual motives, which are far different from what he pretended them to be.

At this point, a miracle occurs. Having brought his pretense up from the subconscious to the conscious level — as shocking as it is — he crashes through. *Awareness of his pretense destroys it — and away fall all the weariness and guilt that goes with pretense.* Because the man no longer identifies with the stage performer, because he sees that the actor is not his True Self, he separates from it. Then, he is forever free, just as an actor playing the dreadful Mr. Hyde separates from the role to become the real and compassionate Dr. Jekyll.

Don't think all this is complicated. It is really very simple. A crisis of pain or suffering should be valued. Not that such things should be self-induced, but, when they come, they must be seen as opportunities. Suffering, when properly used, is the very ending of suffering. Use anguish to eliminate its own cause!

"I don't understand. You say that awareness of anxiety dissolves it. I know how anxious I am and still it persists."

"*Feeling* anxiety is not the same as *awareness* of it. When you merely feel anxious, you are identified with it;

113

you are so close you can't see it. If you close your eyes and feel a round object with your fingers, you may worry that it is a bomb. Open your eyes and you see it is a harmless ball. Likewise, as we awaken to see things as they really are, our pains disappear."

Krishnamurti explains correct awareness:

> Awareness is observation without condemnation. Awareness brings understanding, because there is no condemnation or identification but silent observation. If I want to understand something, I must observe, I must not criticize, I must not condemn, I must not pursue it as pleasure or avoid it as a non-pleasure. There must merely be the silent observation of a fact. There is no end in view but awareness of everything as it arises.[2]

## Suffering Has No Power Over You

Let's clarify our discoveries:

We can either suffer from our suffering, or we can use it to end suffering. To abolish anguish we must understand its nature. What is suffering? It is a face to face encounter with something that the false self doesn't want to face. It is resistance against the Truth, against Reality. We resist the very Truth that could liberate us because we don't recognize it, because we are still under the delusion that falsehood is all there is.

Suffering is nothing more than an attempt by Nature to help us face illusions we don't even suspect we harbor. Scientist Louis Agassiz points out, "Nature brings us back to absolute truth whenever we wander." If we learn the lesson, we lose both the illusion and the pain it causes. If we resist, misery remains.

"If our pains are caused by wrong ideas, why do we fight so fiercely whenever a mystic tries to separate us from them?"

---

[2] J. Krishnamurti, *The First and Last Freedom* (New York: Harper & Row, Publishers, Inc., 1954).

"Because there is a temporary and frightening gap between the old and the new. You resist leaving prison because you fear that the other world may be even worse. People fight inner liberty because their prison-conditioned minds project anxious imaginations of what the new world is like. But it is not at all like prison. You must have courage to leave the pseudo-security of your prison-thinking. Then you experience the happy new."

Suffering *of itself* teaches us nothing, any more than boarding a ship takes us anywhere. We must use it correctly. We must endure it long enough to call its bluff. We must not run away to refuge in self-pity or to high-sounding rationalizations. Such retreats only increase the illusion that suffering has us on the run. In spiritual battle we defeat the enemy, not through flight but through standing still long enough to see that we have mistakenly attributed power to the enemy. Suffering has no power over anyone. Just perceive this. Perceive it and you win every time, whether the assault comes as loneliness, frustration, despair, whatever.

Do not think of suffering as something hateful or something to escape. To do this is to miss the meaning entirely.

*Learn to use suffering wisely.*

For what purpose?

*To dissolve the very suffering.*

As a practical illustration, suppose our distress is caused by a cruel remark from someone. Now, the distress arises because the remark fell on the false self, whose very nature is touchy, sensitive, indignant. But as this artificial self fades away through psychological insight, what entity is left to suffer? If a thousand people throw black paint against the air, it remains clear and undisturbed.

## What a Mystic Knows

"You say we must react rightly to suffering. What is a wrong reaction?"

"When you resist it, hate it, fight it, try to escape it with some frantic exterior activity."

"Why are those reactions wrong?"

"Because they prevent you from understanding the whole process. And that is why you suffer over and over again. If your car breaks down, do you walk away and pretend there's nothing wrong, or do you work at understanding the mechanical failure in order to repair it? Why not face the inner breakdown and correct it? Unsolved pain gradually increases."

"In what way?"

"Take a person who gets angry frequently. He justifies his painful anger by saying that people are rude or inconsiderate to him; therefore, he has a right to his anger. He fails to see that anger is a self-punishing feature of the ego-self, which can, if he chooses, be dissolved. So, by not handling his anger correctly, he creates other negativities that go with it, like guilt and tiredness."

"That is true. I see that much."

"When a man reaches a certain level of insight, he takes an entirely different view of his unhappiness. He no longer resists or resents it. He understands its value. He sees that a shock or crisis is a message telling him that in some way he is living out of harmony with his original nature. Therefore, although shocked, he studies what happened. As his enlightenment grows, he is less and less shocked and more and more at peace."

"I will try to understand."

"Good. You will be happy. But don't expect your friends to grasp this. They are still resisting everything that happens to them!"

Here we can add another definition of the true mystic:

He is one who has suffered just as much as anyone,

maybe a lot more, but he faced it squarely; he entered deeply into the dark tunnel and came out on the other side.

The mystic understands the sufferer and has great compassion for him. The mystic knows how much this man or that woman secretly agonizes — and he knows the cure. But he also understands the tremendous resistance within the sufferer. This is why the enlightened teacher never argues about spiritual matters; he sees the uselessness of trying to persuade the unpersuadable.

What is the mystic's attitude toward those who refuse to receive the very truth that could set them free? It is very simple. He says to them silently, "When the pain becomes unbearable, when you are willing to give up the false self, come back and we'll talk it over."

## The Authentic Answer to Worry

What about that type of pain we call worry?

It is totally unnecessary.

This is not a beautiful dream. It is a fact. When you reach a certain height of wakefulness you don't worry about anything — and I mean *anything*.

One of the deepest despairs of man is that he can do nothing about the thousand and one worries that his day dishes out. He sighs, "Well, that's life," never realizing that all can be different.

To find the answer, we must return to the basic fact of man's real self and his invented self. The false self, with all its wrong viewpoints, can do nothing to dismiss worry; it can only cause it. The conditioned mind can only substitute a new worry for an old one, like a motorist slipping in a muddy field from one mess to another.

Let us not be fooled by thoughtless thinking on this point. No man who still lives from his false self is free from worry. The only way you or I, or anyone else finds freedom is by extinguishing the false sense of "I" and living from our authentic nature.

Let's state the problem as simply as possible: All worry — and there are no exceptions — all worry springs from false notions about ourselves. We mistakenly think we must be popular — and, when the telephone fails to ring, we worry. We assume that we must be wise — and, when we do some foolish thing, we fret over our intelligence. We insist that exciting things should happen to us — and, when they don't, we feel empty.

It is utter nonsense that we must be popular, or wise, or excited. We need be only one thing — mature, and decent, and happy human beings. Then, by one of the magical features of mysticism, we are genuinely wise and excited in a new way.

You no longer take anxious thought for tomorrow. You are carefree and cheery. You won't know nor care where your good comes from. And for advanced students of the Mystic Path I add this: Not only will you neither know nor care where your good comes from but you won't care whether it comes or not. You already have it.

Two farmers own wells. The well of the first farmer is dry. He gets water only when rainfall fills it accidentally and irregularly. That farmer is insecure and apprehensive; he is at the mercy of chance. The well of the second farmer is fed naturally and constantly by an underground stream. That farmer is relaxed and unworried.

When living from our True Source, we are relaxed and unworried.

## To end heartache and suffering

1. Study suffering scientifically.

2. All heartache is caused by wrong viewpoints.

3. We must stop running imaginative, negative films.

4. By bringing anguish up to full awareness, we destroy it once and for all.

5. Like the hunter in the story, you can rise to the top of life.

6. Awareness means simply understanding ourselves. We must work sincerely at self-awareness.

7. Review the supplied *Lights Along the Mystic Path*.

8. Every crisis of pain can be used to make future pain impossible.

9. Do not resist any kind of anguish or heartache. If we resist, we miss the very lesson it teaches.

10. Worry is nonexistent to the advanced traveler along the Mystic Path.

# 8

# Mystical Mysteries
# That Change
# Your Life

Author and mystic, P. D. Ouspensky, wrote an interesting novel called the *Strange Life of Ivan Osokin*. Ivan, a young man who finds life intolerable, visits a wise magician to complain, "If only I could go back through the years and start again. If only I could do things differently." The magician assures him that it would not make the slightest difference — he would repeat the very same mistakes. In disbelief, Ivan asks to be sent back for a test. Agreeing, the magician sends Ivan back twelve years.

Ivan goes through the very same dismal experiences. Everything tragic that happened before happens again. He is amazed to find that, in spite of all his good intentions, he has no power to alter the course of his life. Ivan returns to the magician in complete bewilderment to ask what it is all about. The magician explains: For events to be different,

Ivan himself must be different. His very inward nature must be transformed, made new. A new nature, which calls for persistent self-work, will set new causes into motion for him. Then, everything will be different.

The Mystic Path leads to total transformation of our reactions toward life. How amazing it really is. Everything is seen in a different light. What we previously thought vital becomes trivial; what we used to ignore, we now treasure. We see that riotous social conditions need not mean disturbance within *us*. We clearly realize that freedom's inner kingdom cannot be touched by exterior attacks.

We delightedly perceive that we can truly choose to change from victim to victor. We can stop running so frantically through our day, for we understand that we really did not want to race so breathlessly; we merely did not know what else to do. But now we know. We have caught that first magnificent glimpse of a higher world.

We also sense the secret of continued progress: We need only refuse to accept our present vision of this new World as the limit of the World.

## A Life-Changing Technique

In our everyday affairs we clearly see the need for placing things in their right order. We know the foundation of a home must come before the roof; we realize we must trim the vegetables before cooking them. The very same principle of the right order of things must prevail in our psychic life if we are to avoid confusion and achieve success.

This single idea, faithfully understood and applied, could mark the turning point of your life.

A man wants to be happy. Fine. He can be happy. But, if he places happiness as his first order of business, he will not find it. He will find temporary thrills or distractions, but not abiding contentment. He must proceed in the right order. Happiness *follows* a sincere effort at self-discovery.

We cannot possibly be happy, if we are strangers to ourselves. Self-understanding is the door to quietude.

Let's see how it goes in other areas:

- *Change yourself, rather than working to change others.*
- *Place the inner man in control of the outer.*
- *Abandon the false before seeking the true.*
- *Be loving and you will be loved.*
- *Attend to the reason why you felt hurt, not to those who hurt you.*
- *Set inner integrity before good works.*
- *Place thinking before speaking.*
- *Be a real person, then a social person.*
- *Understand yourself, then try to know others.*
- *Set self-awareness before self-gratification.*
- *Destroy negative attitudes, not negative conditions.*
- *Place small efforts before great determinations.*

Maybe you face an unexpected and disturbing crisis. What is the right order to meet this crisis? Do not attack it directly. That only makes it worse. Rather, immediately connect it with everything you know about the Mystic Path. Suppose you feel that your life is shallow, spinning in pointless circles. What does the Mystic Path say? Well, it says you feel this way only because you have not as yet returned to your original nature. Also, it tells you to seek more self-knowledge. It gently points out that such despair is totally unnecessary. And so on. All this leads to the answer — but it will be entirely different from what you now imagine!

Remember your purpose in working with the principles of the Mystic Path. You want a change of being. Do not practice merely to have something to do. Your goal is a new self.

"Please discuss the right order of things in connection with our physical appetites. We overeat; we're obsessed with sex."

"Physical appetites in themselves are normal. You are enslaved when you place your *gratification* of them before your *understanding* of them. We are slaves to whatever we don't understand. Food and sex are powerful stimulants. Stimulation is a craving of the false self. People fear that by losing these cravings they will be left with nothing to live for. In truth, they will have something for which to live for the first time."

The supreme right order was clearly presented hundreds of years ago: Seek first the Kingdom of Heaven and all else will be added to you.

## How to Be Loving

We live in a universe governed by spiritual and psychological principles. We have nothing to do but understand and ally ourselves with them. This was the entire foundation of the philosophy of Baruch Spinoza, a Dutch mystic.

We start by realizing that our deeper self already knows and understands. Like a powerful underground spring seeking to burst above ground, so do life-principles seek to break through our hardened attitudes. As we permit the breakthrough, things that have puzzled us for years clear up. We see why everything happened to us the way it did.

Take the principles governing love between man and woman. The ability to give love and to receive it are equal. A man can offer a woman genuine love but, unless she is on the same level of love, she can neither receive nor reciprocate.

We cannot receive anything above our own level any more than we can stand on the ground and reach a peach at the top of the tree.

There is no point whatever in an unloving man searching around for a woman to love him. He will meet endless frustration. In the first place, he would not recognize a genuinely loving woman if he met one. Secondly, a loving woman would wisely see that she and the man had nothing in common. A love relationship between two people of widely separated psychic levels is impossible. There is no attraction between them. Like attracts like. Love can only be attracted by and returned by love.

Another principle to bear in mind is that the false self has no real existence. But because we wrongly assume that we are this artificial self, we confusedly act from it. It is as if a man put on a gorilla suit and, unthinkingly, assumed that he really was a gorilla. By thinking and acting from that false premise, he behaves awkwardly wherever he goes. Consciousness of his true identity makes the gorilla-in-man fall away, permitting him to behave skillfully. When the Mystic Path asks us to give up our false sense of self, it asks only that we give up our awkwardness.

Living in harmony with universal principles can be compared with playing the piano. We know when we are following the music and we know when we strike a wrong note. We can hear the difference immediately. Likewise, when feeling discord in our lives, we know we have failed to play the cosmic composition correctly. But the disharmony need not continue. We were not made for failure. We can look again and practice some more. We can learn to play it rightly.

"You once said that mysticism is a system for mental health. I imagine a grasp of its principles helps us to think clearly."

"We learn to see things as they really are, not as we imagine they are. For example, we must stop associating change with loss. Notice how you fear that change will take things away from you? Psychologically, change is never a loss; it is change only. Watch how your world brightens as you let this idea enter your daily events."

## Your Four Golden Keys

Yes, there will be times when we get weary. Our studies, books and seekings may seem futile. Expect it to happen; it happens to everyone on the Path. For one thing, we are governed by the principle of alternating effort-and-relaxation. A change of pace is necessary for refreshment. When tiredness or discouragement sets in, don't be upset. Quietly set the books aside and have some tea and cake. Have no fear in doing this. If the intention is right, we are naturally drawn back again to our studies, revived, and ready for the next upward step.

All we need is a decision to seek the light. When that is done, all else is done for us.

A sign of deepening insight: When you see how one psychological principle connects with another. You might, for example, see how "Resist not evil" connects with the law of not worshiping false gods. How? When we resist something, perhaps an unkind remark, the very resistance implies a belief that that remark can harm us. We are, therefore, worshiping a false and powerless god — the unkind remark. Nonresistance calls the bluff and destroys the falsity.

The first step toward harmonizing with universal laws is to hear of them. Let me present four simple and basic steps which readers found helpful in my previous book, *Psycho-Pictography*. Called "Your Four Golden Keys to New Freedom and Happiness," they are:

1. *A sincere desire for inner change:* Self-transformation begins from the moment we earnestly wish to be a different kind of person.

2. *Contact with workable principles:* We must connect ourselves with a source of genuine help, perhaps a book, or an enlightened teacher, or with our own inner light.

3. *Self-honesty:* We must heroically face the facts about ourselves, even if disturbing, in order to break the chains.

4. *Persistence:* With endurance, happiness comes gradually but definitely, like a blinking light that finally glows permanently.[1]

As we read and work with mystic principles found in a book, we experience a mysterious change within. What we formerly took as attractive words and phrases now turns into a very definite *feeling*. This means that we have seen beyond the words; the intuitive self has broken through to transform an intellectual idea into a living experience.

It is as though you attend a lecture by a famous astronomer who tells you about the wonders of the moon. He explains its size, distance from the earth, and so on. You absorb the facts, but they do not excite you emotionally. Then, as the lecture ends, you step outside to look directly at the brilliantly yellow moon. What a difference between the words and the experience!

## The Mystery of Tao

Out of the East drifts that mystical fascination known as Tao. At first glance, it appears too airy a philosophy for the modern man bustling around his cash registers and space rockets. But wait a minute. Let's look. We don't want to miss anything.

Taoism, which means *The Way*, was founded by the ancient mystic, Lao-tse. Years later, his teachings were explained and expanded by his chief follower, Chuang-tse.

What is it? What does it have to say to busy people? No system is more to the point than Tao: Life is a series of natural and spontaneous changes. Don't resist them; don't wish things were different. That only creates sorrow. Go along. Let Reality be Reality. Let things flow naturally forward in whatever way they like. Be like a pebble carried effortlessly along the stream of life.

---

[1] Vernon Howard, *Psycho-Pictography: The New Way to Use the Miracle Power of Your Mind* (West Nyack, N.Y.: Parker Publishing Company, 1965).

Why? Why, that is the way to harmony. It is the little ego-self that vainly thinks it controls nature. It doesn't. It doesn't need to. But every time it tries, it fails and cries. How strange that we should even ask why we should not interfere with the course of events. Why, that is the only road to what we really want — a quiet garden in the midst of a rowdy world.

Tao points out, "The snow goose need not bathe to make itself white. Neither need you do anything but be yourself."

Riches? Fame? Power? How empty. With Tao, you have genuine wealth that never fades away. And you don't need to shout it around. If you have a pocketful of gold, it is just as valuable whether others know about it or not.

"But," the bustling man protests, "we can't just drift. We must take the initiative; we must do something."

I can almost hear Lao-tse's gentle reply, "Yes, I am afraid that's your whole problem. You are always doing something. In your anxiety to gain a goal, or relieve a pressure, you do something impulsive. So you create a second problem. Slow down. Don't fear to be without an immediate solution. Let your receptive mind supply the answer. It is just as useless and unnatural to work at living as it is to force a ball to roll downhill."

Too different from the usual? Let's see. Don't resist life, says Lao-tse. So does Christ. See the folly of egotistical strivings, urges Tao. So does the New Testament, and William James, and Arthur Schopenhauer, and Erich Fromm, and Albert Schweitzer, and Henry David Thoreau — plus anyone else who has at least glimpsed the lofty life.

Peace and contentment, in spite of the noisy world. That is the simple message of Tao. Nothing airy about *that*.

Try it. Make the following experiment for the next thirty minutes: Let life happen. Just let it happen. Let anything happen the way it wants, with no resistance and no objection. Go about as if you need not think about anything. Your first surprise will be that your usual duties go on very nicely as before. Secondly, you will catch a grand glimpse of the effortlessly flowing of Tao. You do not carry; you are carried.

## Where to Find Lasting Loyalty

"You frequently say that we can live in this rough world without getting roughed up. I really don't see how this can be so."

"An illustration will help. If you ride an airplane along rough ground, you get bumped. If you fly above the bumps, they are still there for other people, but they cannot jolt you. You are carried aloft by a new sense of self."

"But what if I get jolted in the meantime?"

"Be encouraged by this principle: Any shock or tragedy, when met with self-awareness, can never again shock with the same intensity and will eventually disappear altogether."

"What is an example of useful shock or tragedy?"

"Loss. Whenever a man loses something of value he suffers a degree of shock. He should then work with and rely upon the mystical principles he has absorbed. He can then come out upon a higher level than before. Everything depends upon the right use of shock. Rightly used, we loosen the chains; wrongly used, they grow tighter. Suppose you lose someone important to your happiness. You gain strength by seeing that you were depending upon external values which have no permanency. Maybe you lose popularity or power. Become aware that you were using them for a needless sense of identity. Correctly used, shock diminishes future shock."

Notice that our human level of living goes from one betrayal to another. Look at it. You cling to youth and are betrayed by advancing years. Your wealth and position threaten to leave you at any moment. Your ambitions and your careers show treachery by keeping you anxious over them. Your relatives and friends betray you by changing or disappearing or quarreling.

It is not negative to face all this. It is tremendously positive. It means that the yearning you have for something far better can now be heeded. Having been betrayed long enough on the human level, you are ready for that lofty level where loyalty only exists.

There is a technique for winning all this. Simply stated, the technique is this: We must cease to know so many wrong things. We must willingly let go of the vanity and pride that pretends it has already won. The exit of the false makes room for the true. A Sufi mystic sums up:

*Sell your cleverness and buy bewilderment;*
*Cleverness is mere opinion, bewilderment is intuition.*
— Jalal-Uddin Rumi

I want to tell you how enormously important all these principles are to you. I am not questioning your intelligence when I say that you may not as yet see how overwhelmingly vital they are to your life. Quietly accept the fact that you may not, as yet, have grasped the magnificence of it all — though it is quite possible that you have had your first grand glimpse.

It is a thousand times more valuable than anything else you now possess. Work to see this. So much — so very much more than you can imagine — depends upon it. These ideas are not my personal opinions. They are far beyond that. They are the very truths that set you free.

## Be of Good Cheer

Many mysteries are solved when we see that life consists of various levels of understanding. Everyone occupies a different level. For one thing, we see that we fail at many things because we try to claim the success of a higher level while still occupying a lower one. That is like trying to claim the contents of an apartment on the sixth story while actually living on the third story. To claim the rewards of a certain level, we must actually be on that level.

We will also see that on a lofty level of living there is no such thing as competition. On the human level of business, and politics, and male-female relations, competition exists. But higher up, there is no such thing. You and everyone else has all and everything needed. Competition and limitation have no meaning. Do any of us compete for the air we breathe? That is how it is up there.

It is urgent for us to see this: Nothing can improve until we see the link between our psychological level and the things that happen to us. If we are secretly blaming people or events for our problems, we miss the mark completely. There is a human cause for everything troublesome, and that cause is the very person who experiences the effect!

Frustration occurs when we try to *do* without first *understanding*. We cannot possibly act successfully above our own level of insight, but we can work to raise the level. Understanding *is* doing, the kind that returns a profit. Do not race ahead of your understanding; let it be like a torch that goes ahead to light up the Path before you.

Here is a mystery to unravel: Each new upliftment must be preceded by a plunge into the darkness, like a train going upward through a tunnel. Why must darkness and uncertainty precede our exit into the sunlight of a higher level? This darkness indicates a willingness to shed vain illusions that we already know this or that. It is a state of honest receptivity to wisdom greater than our own. The time-honored mystical classic, *Theologia Germanica*, explains, "And so his hard-won not-knowing becomes his highest knowledge."

If we insist that we already know what it is like beyond the tunnel, we deceive ourselves. What we imagine will be but a counterfeit manufactured by our conditioned desires.

If we dare the darkness, we find the light. When human

reasoning completely fails to entice answers, they come. We cannot force ourselves to think clearly, but we can become aware that we are *not* in clarity. Consciousness of our confusion then leads to a new kind of clearness in which there is no more doubt. It should not bother us in the slightest to suspect that there might be something wrong with the way we think. To the contrary, it should excite us, for we are on the doorstep to fantastic discoveries.

Be of good cheer. You have often asked yourself whether there is something above and beyond your present routine life. There is. Just as the wind is not meant for enclosure in a room, neither are you meant for confinement within your thoughts and feelings. True living is just as free as the wind.

## Mystical Teachings About the Future

What proceeds from all this? Everything for which you have been searching. I am not speaking merely of spiritual benefits, but of all those down-to-earth reliefs everyone wants.

What do you want for your physical health? Relaxation from muscular tension? No more headaches? Abundance of natural energy? No more exhaustion? Restful sleep? You can have them. Take it as true that you will feel better and stronger. Health-power increases as you step upward to new levels.

There is a story about the small boy attending a party next door to his own home. Seeing a couple of other children depart, he thought it was also time for him to leave. The hostess asked, "What's your hurry?" He thought it over for a moment, then yelled over to his mother, "Mom, what's my hurry?"

That story illustrates another reward — freedom from a nagging sense of anxious haste. Our dawning awareness leads us to ask, "What's my hurry?" Listening carefully, the answer comes, "None at all."

131

And we are unhappy, uneasy, strained, oppressed, and fearful we shall be shallow. For over the margins of life comes a whisper, a faint call, a premonition of richer living which we know we are passing by. Strained by the very mad pace of our daily outer burdens, we are further strained by an inward uneasiness, because we have hints that there is a way of life vastly richer and deeper than all this hurried existence, a life of unhurried serenity and peace and power. If only we could slip over into that Center! [2]

We can slip over into that Center. Any time we really choose.

Another benefit connects with the future. The question comes, "Does the Mystic Path enable us to foresee our future, or is prophecy a fake?"

"There is authentic prophecy by which you can foretell your *inner* future. By working at self-transformation, you can accurately predict easy living. As for outer events, you need pay no attention to them beyond your normally intelligent plans. When living from your True Self, you have no concern with future finances or friendships. You truly take no thought for tomorrow. The new Cause within you makes everything right without unnatural effort on your part."

"What does the Mystic Path tell us about heaven?"

"Heaven is not a place; it is a lofty level of psychic development. Love is heaven. So is peace, understanding, compassion, tenderness. Hell is also a psychic condition; one of ignorance and unawareness. Hatred is hell. So is anger, arrogance, jealousy, competitiveness, and especially fear. Heaven or hell are right now — as you well know without me even telling you. You get your first foot into heaven by courageously facing the fact that you presently have none of its peace."

---

[2] Thomas R. Kelly, *A Testament of Devotion* (New York: Harper & Row, Publishers, Inc., 1941).

"I have at least a glimpse of my own pretenses. How can I stop?"

"A small child imitates a famous soldier or great Indian chief, but at maturity he finds no pleasure in artificial roles. He yearns for his real self. As he heads toward it he stops playing great-man, or famous-man, or dynamic-man. Then, he loses the torment in playing these shallow roles. Try to see that you *are* acting; then, the costume falls away of itself."

## How to Work for Yourself Profitably

People are puzzled over the part they should play in transforming their lives. They say, "Where must I make a personal effort and where should I be still and receptive to the truth?"

Never forget, receptivity *is* your personal effort. It is the whole works. You must not try to do anything else, for, in fact, you *can't* do anything else. If we, standing in darkness, do our part by opening the door, the light rushes in to meet us.

Receptivity has many interesting areas. For example, our protests and objections to a truthful statement make a fine source for self-study. Notice how quick we are to object, and deny, and argue, whenever a new idea presents itself. We may think that we argue because we already know the truth, when, in fact, honest reflection reveals the exact opposite: we protest because our artificialities are threatened with exposure. This could lead to the honest insight, "Well, I'm not as sure as I thought. Here is an opportunity to crack through my false ideas."

As strange as it seems, receptivity means that you don't take anybody's word for anything. You think for yourself. There is a counterfeit form of receptivity which is nothing more than gullibility. Some people take anybody's word for anything. This is mental laziness, and what a painful price is paid. But refusing to be gullible does not mean that we become cynical. It means we must test everything for ourselves.

You often read a story or see a film going like this: The hero sets out to accomplish some noble task, such as carrying life-saving medicine to a remote jungle tribe. Every step calls for super-heroism: his mission is blocked by jealous officials, or he is threatened by jungle storms, or he is foolishly attacked by the very natives he hopes to help. But he persists and wins. We admire him.

Our admiration is our awakened sense of nobility. We know that the true hero must often stand alone, must persist in spite of danger from foolish men, that he must prefer integrity to popularity, goodness to applause.

The Mystic Path calls for the bravest and best within us. Uprightness. Integrity. Honesty. Fearlessness. That is all. There is nothing complex about success.

Make up your mind to go all the way. Do not hesitate. Do not compromise. Place the Truth above all else. Do not be afraid. The most helpful obstacles are the insurmountable ones.

And don't apologize. You need apologize for nothing. You are a free and dignified human being. Whether aware of it or not, you *are*.

> *I do not trouble my spirit to vindicate itself or be understood; I see that the elementary laws never apologize....*
>
> — Walt Whitman

It is all very simple. If you will really fight for yourself, you will win.

## *Helpful ideas from this chapter*

1. Inward transformation magically changes everything else.

2. Place first things first.

3. Work to understand spiritual and psychological principles, for example, love attracts love.

4. Remember the Four Golden Keys supplied in this chapter.

5. Let life happen. Flow with it. Live effortlessly.

6. Try to see the connection between your level of understanding and the things that happen to you.

7. Be of good cheer!

8. The future is all good to the person who conscientiously works upon his inner life.

9. Open the door of your mind to positive ideas and impressions.

10. Walk along the Mystic Path accompanied by the bravest and best within you.

# 9

# The Sure Cure
# for Fear
# and Tension

"I think I could tackle my problem more wisely if I could see what it is. Isn't it strange that I don't know what's bothering me? I used to think I understood, but no longer. Do you have insight into this? Do you know what my problem is?"

"Yes, I know."

"Will you point it out?"

"If you are deeply interested in the exploration. It is a psychological law that no one can be given anything that they don't really want. Do you want a thorough discussion?"

"Yes. I somehow sense that this is the only way. So tell me, please, what is my basic difficulty?"

"You are afraid."

"Afraid? Really?"

"Fear is always a dominating difficulty of anyone separated

from his original nature. Just as thorns are natural to a cactus, so are fear and anxiety a part of the false self. But there is bright hope here. Do you see it?"

"By recovering our natural self, we lose our fears. Is that what you mean?"

"Yes. Anxiety becomes impossible."

"That's what I want. So, please, I'd like to explore it."

That is what we will do in this chapter. Everyone treading the Mystic Path must slay the dragons of fear, both the surface shakings and the deeper dreads. Fear is not only a terrible foe in itself but leads to other negativities, such as anger, which Confucius described as a foremost self-destroyer.

The very root of fear is a false sense of identity. All other negative states, like worry and restlessness, grow from this, just as sour apples spring from an unhealthy tree. Man wrongly assumes that he is his name, or body, or possessions. Because of this, he fearfully fights through life trying to prove that he is these things. This is utterly futile — as men sadly discover every day. Because they don't see the alternative, they continue the vain struggle. And so you see millions of people acting gaily but their eyes tell quite another story.

Living from this false sense of identity creates thousands of fearful and self-damaging ideas toward life. For instance, there is no more dangerous, nor frustrating, doctrine than that "you ought" to live according to the dictates of a confused society. You ought to do nothing of the sort. In fact, the only *real* life you have is that which springs spontaneously from your own spiritual nature.

When this life is achieved, we are no longer mechanical robots but noble human beings *who live as we really want to live.* No longer do we march dully to the blaring bands of an authoritarian society, but we dance gaily to the music swelling up from our original being. In that free state we are unafraid of anything or anyone — *anything or anyone.*

## The Tremendous Discovery of Socrates

One deeply rooted anxiety that must be abolished has been expressed in the phrase, "But what will happen to me tomorrow?" People strain over their future finances, friendships, health, just about everything. They hope they will improve, or at least not worsen. But the hope is fearful, for they sense their lack of control over the future.

Away with all this self-torture. I tell you truly that you need not have the slightest concern with tomorrow. All is well. Even if you do not realize it, the fact remains. But you must not try to feel this fact, for your emotions will fool you. Without involving your feelings, simply see the fact that all is well. By doing this, you create the legitimate and abiding feeling of assurance. The right order is to place fact before feeling.

Perhaps someone asks, "But does all this apply to me as an individual? Can I personally know the answers?"

You can. You can certainly establish yourself upon the unshakeable rock of your True Self. Yes, of course, the answers come to the man or woman who inquires with this kind of earnestness:

> I would rather have trustworthy and satisfying answers to these questions than all the gold of the Indies. To *know* — not to believe, not to hope, not to have faith, but to *know* that the universe is friendly, that our feet are set on an intelligent pilgrimage, and there is Love at the heart of things: this is knowledge for which I am still questing and for which I would gladly barter, as for the pearl of great price, all other knowledge.[1]

It is helpful to see that those who attain the lofty life have the same experiences. The Mystic Path presents the same challenges — and rich rewards — to all. Everyone meets baffling questions which seem unanswerable. Discouragement and a sense of futility are common to all.

---

[1] Raynor C. Johnson, *The Imprisoned Splendour* (New York: Harper & Row, Publishers, Inc., 1953).

But all who persist, arrive. Let's examine the experiences of two enlightened men; these serve as heartening examples.

When Socrates reached his fortieth year, his perplexities about himself reached their peak: "What is life all about? What is really worthwhile? Who is this person called Socrates? Is there another way to live?"

Socrates put his questions to men who supposedly knew the answers — the educators, philosophers, politicians, men of skill, and men in authority. Their muddled replies proved that they were just as ignorant as he. But there was a difference. Socrates *knew* he was ignorant, while they, in their human conceit, perfectly believed in the mythical self-pictures they had of themselves as wise counselors. So Socrates resolutely set out to do what every psychic explorer must do — seek the truth for himself, within himself. Seeking, he found. He came up with the declaration, "The unexamined life is not worth living."

Compare Socrate's quest with that of Count Tolstoy's in Chapter 2. Notice how their intense inner integrity compelled them to see through the shallow authorities of the day and to plunge into the mystery for themselves. Though widely separated by centuries, Socrates and Tolstoy reached the same tremendous conclusion: "To find yourself, think for yourself."

## The Strange Truth about Results

"I'm both fascinated and baffled by something you said the other night. You said we must learn to be completely unconcerned with the results of our social and business efforts. Of all the mystical principles you have given us, this is the hardest to grasp."

The inquirer is right. While it takes intensive study, no mystical truth offers more enrichment. It is vital that we do not misunderstand, so let's explore carefully.

Learn to be indifferent to the results of your efforts in

the human affairs of moneymaking, friendships, career, and so forth.

Notice the tormenting worry over results. Will the new friends like us? Can I make the sale? Will my marriage be happy? Can I succeed at this? Concern with results is a major torture to man. Moreover, *it is the very thing that unconsciously causes failure.*

Meet both so-called good results and so-called bad results with quiet indifference. Neither makes any difference *as far as your personal happiness is concerned.*

We demand a financial success, or a social gain, because we think it will fulfill us inwardly. It won't. It never will — as we have suspected all along. So-called success provides ego-excitement, but never self-fulfillment. It is just as impossible for an exterior result to provide inner happiness as it is for a new hat to give us a new mind.

A man may object, "But what do I have to live for, if not for exciting results?" The mystic replies, "For abiding happiness."

I know. This principle goes against everything we have been taught. All of us are conditioned from birth to insist, expect, demand — and be anxious. Yes, this is the human way. But we are tired of it. We are on the esoteric path where everything is different. The difference is the gift of cheery abandonment for which we have always yearned.

When we don't have an ego-centered demand for a particular result, we remain lighthearted, whether the outcome is so-called good or so-called bad. The free man dwells above human good and bad; he floats in a higher Good.

Not that we are careless in our human affairs. Far from it. We are much more skillful in running our daily tasks. This freedom clears the mind, turns emotions into allies. (See Chapter 10 for more details on this idea.)

Think of some plan that you desperately want to

succeed. Now ask yourself, "How would I feel if I didn't care how it turned out?" See! Your peace is assured, regardless of results. That is what we are getting at.

"I am a practical business executive. I don't see how I can be indifferent to results in the arena of dollars and cents. This particular idea somehow eludes me."

"Let's put it this way: Be just as active as you like in your business, but do it to earn your living, *never for ego-gratification.* Try to see the difference in the two. I guarantee that you will never again have a business headache, not even when severe problems arise. The situation may be confused, but *you* are not."

## Let Cosmic Principles Work for You

"I'd like that. Will you please summarize?"

"Intelligently work for this or that goal in your daily affairs, but give up all concern for results. Let whatever wants to happen go ahead and happen. You keep your peace when you don't demand a certain result; for example, that the customer *should* buy your product, or that this person *should* appreciate you. Set up no demands for anything from anyone. Grasp this tremendous principle and your life will never again be the same."

You, the reader, can start right now. Try it in small matters at first. Do what you like, but leave results entirely to themselves. Call it an outcome, but do not label it as either a good or bad outcome. By doing this, you work in harmony with mysterious and powerful cosmic principles. Now, let's discover a practical procedure for effective work.

Over the years I have found it a valuable practice to select a basic principle, reduce it to a single sentence, and reflect on it for several days. We do this in our Mystic Path Study Groups. You can do likewise with any of the hundreds of ideas in this book. Select one that attracts you in particular and work with it. Let's select three mystical principles and see how our reflections might go.

PRINCIPLE: *The Mystic Path calls for courage and persistence.*

MY REFLECTION: "I work daily to become a stronger and more self-aware person. I will be neither surprised nor afraid if and when my present world of beliefs and opinions comes tumbling down. This is both good and necessary. Now, on the cleared space, I can build a new self made of wisdom and quietude."

PRINCIPLE: *Man is asleep, but can awaken.*

MY REFLECTION: "Man suffers because he does not see the true nature of things. So great is his sleep-hypnosis that he doesn't even suspect that he sees everything through the screen of his own false assumptions. But man can wake up! All can be changed. There is another world. Through willingness to surrender the ego-self — not through strength or wisdom, but through willingness — he can break free into spontaneous living."

PRINCIPLE: *We must constantly seek a clear self-understanding.*

MY REFLECTION: "Self-clarity comes first. Unless I am clear within myself, I cannot prevent problems from arising, nor can I dismiss them. I must wash away confusing emotions, like depression and self-pity, which make self-clarity impossible. How can we see things clearly when our eyes are full of tears?"

## The Winning Way

One permanent enrichment given by universal principles is a flexibility that enables us to meet and handle any situation. If it is an unwanted habit, it falls away. If it is a family crisis, we remain in calm command.

A person living from his false self cannot do this. He reacts rigidly and mechanically to everything. He has no choice; he must obey the tyrannical dictates of the artificial self, which leads to distress and disaster. This explains the repeated failure of the person who vows not to lose his temper any more and to be nicer to others. The false self cannot be anything but negative. "It is foolish to be surprised when the fig tree produces figs." (Marcus Aurelius)

A rigid man is like a lecturer who writes out ten speeches but is satisfied only with the last one. Since he carelessly carries the nine jumbled versions with him as he faces his audience, he fumbles around, reads the wrong notes, forgets what he wants to say, and so on. He is embarrassed and distressed, all because he is still connected with the faulty material of the past. Yet, he can use his intelligence so that this won't happen again. He can toss out the wrong notes. Then he can speak accurately and easily.

So can we, by dismissing the false ideas we have collected over the years, be free and flexible.

One useless idea is that a mere discussion of our faults, that is, merely talking about them, does any good. Self-confession must be accompanied by self-insight. Without insight, talk becomes an endless procession of wrongdoing and confession, misbehaving and admitting. Genuine confession represents an honest breakthrough into ourselves. When that happens, there is less and less of wrongdoing and, quite naturally, less pain in the form of reactions. The New Testament term *metanoia*, sometimes translated as "repentance," means "change of mind." That is what we gain as we see into ourselves. We experience genuine change of mind, a new kind of mind, one that is flexible, wise, unafraid, one capable of serving our true interests.

Another false notion to dismiss is that we are threatened by our past follies. Listen! Once we determine to find ourselves, past experiences turn to profit. This includes everything unhappy, sinful, shameful, childish, impulsive, regretful. How? One way to know this is by contrasting what we used to be and what we are changing into. *Nothing is more encouraging than to see ourselves actually changing our very nature.*

In addition, past events help us to see a basic lesson of the Mystic Path: Human folly is done while in a state of nonawareness, of psychic hypnosis. This encourages us to become more awake, for we see that wakefulness is the true and only answer to human folly. Finally, we see that we can become entirely free of guilt and shame stemming from past behavior. We realize that it was not done by the True Self, but by the artificial self — *which is now fading out.* Who needs a candle in the sunlight?

## Fear Has No Power Whatsoever

Fear toward something gives that something false power over you. The chains which appear to enslave us are made of paper. That is what we must see. For example, the question comes:

"You often repeat that we must see things as they really are, not as we imagine them. May we have an example of this from everyday life?"

"Take a man in middle age or older who suddenly sees that his business affairs have failed, or are only mediocre. His friends are much more successful or are already retired on comfortable pensions. The thought fills him with despair. He feels cheated. That man could change everything in a wink. He need only see things as they are in reality; that is, it makes no difference whatsoever *to his own happiness* whether he succeeds or not. It never did make any difference, but he is still hypnotized by deluded society with all its stupid praise of what it calls success. Incidentally, that man's more successful friends are not nearly as happy as they pretend."

To destroy the false power of fear, a man can start with his human relationships. He can break the paper chains looped around him by society. He can refuse to cringe

144

before the cruel and the domineering and daringly pursue his true individuality. If Ralph Waldo Emerson had not penned anything but the following, he would have left mankind with a resounding battle cry of freedom:

"Society everywhere is in conspiracy against the manhood of every one of its members.... Self-reliance is its aversion.... It loves not realities and creators, but names and customs.... He who would gather immortal palms must not be hindered by the name of goodness, but must explore if it be goodness. Nothing is at last sacred but the integrity of your own mind." *(Self-Reliance)*

We might add: Nothing is at last noble but a human being whose mind is free of fear.

"There is a particular area of social relation that is seldom discussed as it needs to be. I'm speaking of the fear that people have toward each other. Will you comment on this?"

"You must never inwardly consent to a fear relationship with another person. Even if you must live with him or her, you must refuse to be afraid. The techniques of the Mystic Path will help you detach yourself."

"What do you mean by a fear relationship?"

"Where you are not fully at ease. There can be no love or understanding if you are uneasy toward another. It is necessary that you become aware of your anxiety toward him or her. This leads to other insights which gradually set you free."

"Why are we afraid of others?"

"Because we want something from them. The desire can be almost anything — companionship, approval, sex, security. The mistake is this: Not having found the True Self which is free from compulsive desires, we seek gratification from people. This creates fear that we won't get what we want or anxiety that the other person will make us pay dearly for it. All this is terrible torture which you must refuse to endure any longer. With your new insight, all your human relationships are carefree."

## The Unusual George Gurdjieff

Let's meet a modern mystic with some uniquely exciting ideas about escape from psychic prison: George Gurdjieff. Though his early life is veiled in mystery, Gurdjieff was probably born in Alexandropal, in Asia Minor, about 1872. This remarkable and often controversial man spent a dozen years roaming about the East in search of esoteric teachings. He returned with a tremendous wealth of wisdom for the Western world.

Gurdjieff summarized the problem: Mankind is asleep but doesn't know it. So deep is his hypnotic slumber that he does his daily walking and talking, his legislating and marrying in a state of unconsciousness. Actually, the acts are the mechanical acts of hypnotized people. And *that,* Gurdjieff declares, is the simple reason why the world goes from one disaster to another: "Would," he asks, "a *conscious* human being destroy himself through war, and crime, and quarrels? No, man simply knows not what he does to himself."

Hopeless? Not at all. Gurdjieff has supreme optimism. It is the only worthwhile kind of optimism — that based on a personal experience of liberation. "You can," he announces, "wake up. You can turn from a mechanical man into a true individualist who runs his own life. Yes, while here on earth you can be a perfectly conscious and happy person. Love, intelligence, peace will no longer be mere words or theories — they will be *you.*"

How? Just be honest with yourself. That opens the door. Try to see the difference between the person you imagine you are and how you actually are. Oh, it might shock a bit at first, but never mind. You are doing what the mass of men never dare to do: *start the process of inner change of being.*

One day during World War I, Gurdjieff and a newspaper reporter named P. D. Ouspensky met in a small cafe to talk things over. It was a momentous meeting of two great minds. Ouspensky became Gurdjieff's chief disciple and reporter. Between the two of them, an intriguing and practical system for self-awakening came forth. One of their basic principles explains the many and varied I's in a man. The unawakened man is not a unified person. He has dozens of selves within him, each falsely calling itself I. Many philosophers, including George Santayana and David Hume, have also observed how a person switches constantly from one I to another, but Gurdjieff and Ouspensky spoke with the most clarity on the subject.

The many I's within a man explains many mysteries about human nature. For example, a man decides to give up an undesirable habit, but the next day he repeats it again. Why? Because another I has taken over, one that likes the habit and has no intention of giving it up. Or perhaps a woman decides to quit fooling around with her life; she determines to find her real self. She reads a book or two and goes to a few lectures. Then, suddenly, she loses all interest and goes back to her self-defeating behavior. What happened? An entirely different I, one that doesn't want her to wake up, took charge.

Gurdjieff provides a simple solution to this contradictory condition: Become aware of the many I's. Watch how one takes over and then another. Also, see that they do not represent the true you, but consist of borrowed opinions and imitated viewpoints. Such Self-Observation weakens their grip; you eventually find your Real I. That is the New Birth proclaimed by esoteric Christianity.

## Give Special Attention to This Idea

Let's see how anxiety connects with a particular desire within a man: the desire for excitement, thrills, emotional sensations.

The greater an individual's enslavement to thrills, the more he suffers from an unsatisfying and unstable life.

Unhealthy desires can never be satisfied; they are a bottomless basket. We escape our compulsive appetites only when we see them as such. It is a sure sign of escape from the psychic torture chamber when we feel less and less compelled to seek artificial stimulations.

In your practice of Self-Observation, notice how uncomfortable it is to be without excitement, to have nothing happening. Notice how you are always doing something in order to keep the mind and body in motion. We are afraid of coming to a stop, of being empty, of not feeling anything. This fear is based on the illusion that without these excitements we would cease to exist. We cannot imagine who we would be if we did not identify ourselves with agitation. Yes, we actually fear that we would cease to exist. *And this is right; the counterfeit self would cease to exist — which is the very thing that gives you genuine existence, real joy, permanent peace.*

What to do? Refuse to accept emotional excitement as happiness. It is not happiness. It is emotional excitement; it is a counterfeit that betrays you. High emotional flights must always crash.

No, do not think that lack of artificial stimulation means boredom. It means the exact opposite. If only you will work to see this! Boredom is the crash from the high flight. This freedom means the fading of boredom and the appearance of authentic inspiration.

I know that this point bothers a lot of people; it is frequently mentioned at my lectures, so I want to repeat: Do not assume that the abandonment of invented thrills will take all the fun out of life. It puts lasting fun *into* your life, maybe for the very first time. If you really mean business, you are in for the time of your life. You are embarking upon the greatest adventure any man has ever experienced.

Real excitement? You have no idea how exciting it is to observe the gradual but definite appearance of your real self.

## The Sure Cure for Fear and Tension

*Watch narrowly*
*The demonstration of a truth, its birth,*
*And you trace back the effluence to its spring*
*And source within us; where broods radiance vast....*
　　　　　　　　— Robert Browning, *Paracelsus*

The only enduring thrill comes with the awakening of our intuitive self. Nothing else ever has or ever will satisfy. We need only examine our present lives to see that this is so. We always pay a dreadful price when we try to induce feelings of aliveness through ego-directed activities.

We are not speaking, of course, of the normal pleasures of good company or interesting recreation. These are both necessary and legitimate. The point is, we can never really enjoy normal recreations unless we have first awakened to ourselves. The awakened man or woman never falls back into depression when the lively party comes to an end. He goes home with tranquility, not with loneliness.

Can you be without noise and stimulation and not be afraid? Can you be inwardly still, without demanding a distraction from the strange stillness? If so, the fearsome silence turns magically into the peaceful harbor you have been seeking all your life.

## The Peaceful Valley

Recall a vital point for making swift progress: We must read and hear these principles with our intuitive self, not with our rigid intellects. Reading mystical facts with a conditioned mind is like reading a sentence backward — we get words, but no meaning. Meaning comes from within. And meaning is within everyone, including you, the reader.

There is a momentous mystical truth which relieves you of all anxiety: *You are not your conditioned thoughts.* Do you see the significance of this? Stop and consider. You are tense over a family crisis. Where is the tension? The only place it can be — within your own mind. You are exhausted over a financial problem. Look, now, where did the tiredness originate? Not in the problem itself, but within your own anxious thoughts toward it.

Do not identify with your thoughts. Do not think you are your anxious thoughts. You are not. You are entirely separate. See your thoughts as a passing stream which you merely observe; don't jump into that stream and get carried away.

We must reach the place where we actually see that we don't know what we are doing with our lives. We must recognize that we don't know where we are going — and never have! This must be done without anxiety and without emotion, just as we might recognize that we took a wrong turn on the highway. We must see that our human opinions are worthless; they can do nothing for us. When this happens, we are on the edge of a monumental discovery.

"But shouldn't we have our personal opinions about who we are and where we are going?"

"Why should you have opinions about anything whatsoever? Why not seek the facts? Opinions and theories are like riding a merry-go-round: you have an illusion that you are going somewhere. People adopt opinions in an attempt to feel secure, but they provide nothing but nervousness. Instead of covering up human shakiness with a shallow theory, why not let the facts expose and destroy it?"

"How do we find facts?"

"Dare to live without opinions. At first, you feel jittery, like an invalid abandoning his cane, but, later, quietness sets in. The test of whether you really see a fact about life is this: When clearly seen, you feel a great sense of relief."

It is as if a party of travelers in a stormy country decides to scale a high mountain to see whether the other side has a peaceful valley. Each man, in turn, tries to climb to the peak, but failing, supplies his pet theory for failure.

One pessimistic hiker guesses that it is probably just as stormy on the other side. A scholar with lots of book-knowledge delivers a long and boring lecture, which says nothing. The third man lazily sits back and gullibly swallows anything the others say.

But a fourth traveler is practical. He has no use for mere theories. He wants to find out for himself. So he courageously climbs all the way to the top. His reward is the fact itself — there *is* a peaceful valley on the other side.

## *Chapter summary of successful ideas*

1. Fear is totally unnecessary.
2. As we dissolve fear, we live as we really want to live.
3. The only solution to inner tension is contact with the inner Self.
4. Let no one think for you. Think for yourself always.
5. Have no concern whatsoever for results.
6. As outlined, let cosmic principles work for you.
7. Fear has no power at all. See this for yourself by refusing a fear relationship with anyone.
8. It is impossible for a unified person to be anxious.
9. Don't accept emotional thrills as genuine happiness.
10. Regardless of exterior disorder, you can be inwardly carefree.

# 10

## The Mystic Path
## to Lasting
## Happiness

What is the brand of happiness experienced by most men and women? Buddha illustrated the sad state of affairs with a remarkably enlightening story: A traveler was passing through the forest when he was sighted and pursued by a tiger. He fled frantically away until stopped by a cliff. Spying a vine hanging down its side, he lowered himself downward. But the vine was too short for him to reach the ground. Just then he saw another tiger below, growling viciously. Tiger above and tiger below — what could be worse? Hanging there, the man saw a luscious looking strawberry growing on the side of the cliff. Reaching out, he took the strawberry between his fingers, bit into its flavor, and happily exclaimed, "How delicious!"

That is how it is with most people. Caught between the tigers of fear and despair, they find a distracting strawberry

— a new excitement, more money, social success — and call it happiness.

It need not be like that at all. We can get rid of the tigers. Then, we can truly enjoy whatever strawberries life offers.

We must see what happiness is not. It is not exterior activity; that is merely a distraction from inner unhappiness.

What, then, is happiness? The answer is not complex. Happiness is simply a state of inner freedom. Freedom from what? With a bit of self-insight, every individual can answer that question for himself. It is freedom from the secret angers and anxieties we tell no one about. It is freedom from fear of being unappreciated and ignored, from muddled thinking that drives us to compulsive actions, and later, to regrets. It is freedom from painful cravings that deceive us into thinking that our attainment of this person or of that circumstance will make everything right. Happiness is liberty from everything that makes us unhappy.

Happiness is formless; it cannot be fitted into the frame of our demands. We insist upon this wife or husband, this career or achievement, this home, this security, excitement, or distraction. Even if we get our demands, we are no happier than before; we have merely covered our unhappiness. It is still there, and it will inevitably show itself when change occurs. We must break the frame altogether, and just let life happen; then, we enter an amazing new world whose existence we never before suspected.

"For a happy life is joy in the truth." (Augustine)

Quietly question every idea you have about yourself. Ask, "Is it possible that I am an entirely different person than I imagine I am?" Suspect that it might be so.

By doing this, you set a miracle in motion. It is an extraordinary experience of awakening to newness. You get a different feeling toward yourself. You cannot define it, nor need you try. But how definite is this first faint stirring of *something else!* If you dip only a single finger into a great river, you feel its powerful flow at once. That is how it comes to us.

## The Truth About Enduring Happiness

We can correct our understanding by seeing that pleasurable feelings are not at all the same thing as happiness. Notice how feelings of pleasure alternate with pangs of displeasure, much like walking alternately between cool shade and boiling heat. Also notice the vague heaviness and anxiety that lies behind emotional excitement. Sensing its impermanency, we painfully know we must soon search around for another source of artificial stimulation. Pleasurable sensations are like greedy dragons, requiring constant feeding.

But enduring happiness and bliss are entirely different from fleeting pleasures:

> Thus we see that though the true aim of mankind is the avoidance of pain and the attainment of Bliss, yet owing to a fatal error man, though trying to avoid pain, *pursues a deluding something named pleasure, mistaking it for Bliss.* That the attainment of Bliss and not pleasure is the universal and highest necessity is indirectly proved by the fact that man is never satisfied with one object of pleasure. He always flies from one to another. From money to dress, from dress to property, thence to conjugal pleasure — there is a restless continuity. And so he is constantly falling into pain, even though he wishes to avoid it by the adoption of what he deems proper means. Yet an unknown and unsatisfied craving seems ever to remain in his heart.[1]

All this does not deny us the right to enjoy life. It does not take away authentic feelings of delight. It does just the

---

[1] Paramahansa Yogananda, *The Science of Religion* (Los Angeles: Self-Realization Fellowship, 1953).

opposite. By not depending upon fleeting pleasures, we find lasting ones. No one and no circumstance can ever take away this inner gladness.

As a matter of fact, people are much too serious. They mistakenly think that seriousness somehow indicates earnestness. Even their playtime is grim, just as if it is something they *must* do. Have you noticed the strange compulsion lurking beneath many so-called recreations? This playtime is heavy, not springing spontaneously from a free spirit, but from a burdensome sense of duty. We think we are somebodies who have a duty to keep our lives on the go. What a dreadful idea. In reality, we are blithe spirits who must learn to play as such. With this special kind of purposelessness, we find real delight and lasting meaning in life. Genuine mystics are not afraid to be playful and twinkle-eyed men.

"Happiness is one of the marks of the Cosmic Sense." (Richard Maurice Bucke, *Cosmic Consciousness*)

## How to Enjoy Yourself

"I would like to relax and enjoy myself, as you suggest, but I don't know how."

"There is no *how* in enjoying yourself. You just go ahead and do it without plan and without thought. Children have this spontaneity; they have not as yet been ruined by society. Why don't you just go ahead and have a good time? Why explain? Why try to justify it? Why not just run out and play?"

"I don't know...."

"Would you really like to know why you don't?"

"Yes. I can take it."

"You are afraid of enjoying yourself. You have a false sense of guilt, which prevents you from letting go. You feel disloyal to your pretenses, that of being a very earnest and sincere sort of person who has no time for such triviality. Also — I must tell you this — you are not earnest toward life

155

anyway. You are grim and gloomy, but you prefer to call this earnestness. You can be properly earnest only when you have found yourself. Only a self-unified and balanced man can have a good time."

"I'm afraid you're right. I never saw this before."

The above ideas emphasize a major point of mysticism. Self-awakening must be the first and foremost business in anyone's life. Otherwise, he falls into one pit after another without knowing why. To awaken, we must first suspect that we are asleep and that *there is another form of consciousness*. Here is where shock and suffering aid us. They force us to realize that nothing is really right, in spite of all our claims and pretenses. That nudges us out of our psychic slumber.

Let's see why awareness of an unhappy state must precede deliverance from it. Suppose we hear the advice, "Stop believing only what you want to believe." Accurate advice. But it means absolutely nothing, unless a man first suspects that he *is* believing only what he wishes. Otherwise, he will assume that he is not harming his happiness by doing this; he will falsely credit himself with clear thinking. No, we cannot do anything *for* ourselves until we are awake to what we do *against* ourselves. "Those who do not observe the movements of their own minds must of necessity be unhappy." (Marcus Aurelius)

"Now that I've started to awaken a bit, I seem to run into new difficulties I never had before. Why this extra conflict?"

"A man asleep in a canoe drifting downstream toward a dangerous waterfall feels no difficulties. But when he wakes up and sees his danger, he starts paddling against the current. All the false ideas of life resist the man who begins to awaken. This is a good sign, not one to fear."

A single mystical truth like this, clearly understood, is a thousand times more valuable than a head stuffed with vague ideas. If we seek quality first, quantity follows. It is like entering a strange mansion at midnight. We may fumble a bit in finding the light switch to the first room, but once found we locate the next switch much easier. Each room becomes progressively easier until, finally, the whole mansion is illuminated.

## You Are a Receiving Set

We cannot increase our basic happiness by altering exterior conditions like marriage, residence, career. Every attempt to do so only increases the sense of despair. It is the essential self that must be changed. Our level of consciousness must be raised.

"Since this is true, why does almost everyone still try to find happiness in exterior things?"

"Because the truth is not deeply seen and understood. Also, exterior changes give an illusion of newness. But it always wears off. You can easily observe this for yourself."

"The alternative, then, is interior transformation. And this comes through receptivity to mystical principles?"

"As your consciousness grows, you will see that you are not a sending set, as previously assumed, but a receiver. You have nothing to do but welcome the healthy impressions that seek entrance all day long. This brings relief from useless struggle and from false responsibility. Suppose a television set thought it was the sending station. It would be useless. When it plays its correct role of receiver, it functions normally."

"How can we be more receptive?"

"A superb start is to become aware of our own resistance to life-invigorating truths. We always have contradictory reactions toward spiritual facts. Part of us is thrilled, but another part is annoyed, even hostile. You see, the truth disturbs us. It creates conflict between the false self, which doesn't want the truth at all, and the True Self, which yearns for it at any price. Observe your own resistance. That in itself weakens it, makes you alertly receptive."

Here again we see the need for being aware of ourselves, for observing what goes on beneath our surface activities. A person might think, for example, that he is very happy while at a picnic. But, beneath his outer gaiety, he might have dozens of subconscious worries over his finances, or worries about whether others like him or not. A clear awareness of such negativities would destroy them, for the sadness is in the thoughts themselves, not in the finances, or in acceptance by others. We are enslaved by anything we do not consciously see. We are freed by conscious perception.

People mistakenly assume that they could be happy if only this or that exterior condition would change. No. No man or woman is happy — regardless of his exterior prosperities — if he lives from his false self. The invented self is unhappiness itself. This is a fact which can never be successfully contradicted; our daily griefs prove it conclusively.

It goes like this:

*The problem:* Man is unhappy because he lives from his false self.

*The technique:* He honestly observes himself.

*The result:* He finds freedom with his True Self.

*The new state:* Man is happy.

## Happiness Along The Mystic Path

See the difference between thinking *of* the following ideas and thinking *from* them. It is thinking *from* that attracts your good. You are making sure progress toward authentic happiness when you:

1. Sense that there is something far beyond your present experience.
2. *Do not cling to the memory of yesterday.*
3. Proceed upon the fact that nothing is too difficult for you to accomplish.

4. *Get tired of being unhappy.*

5. Determine to live your own life, not the one dictated by hypnotized society.

6. *Don't run so much and so hard.*

7. Make small but definite explorations toward self-awakening.

8. *Become more and more willing to set aside long-cherished personal opinions.*

9. Don't let your intellect stand in the way of your intuition.

10. *Cease to blame others for your difficulties and see their source in personal psychic sleep.*

11. Realize that mere physical motion does nothing to construct inner castles.

12. *Become a more self-aware and self-directed individual.*

13. Refuse to compromise with the Truth.

14. *Understand that all you really need is more inner illumination.*

15. See that no one on earth can harm the essential you.

16. *Honestly face your inner poverty as a means of discovering your inner wealth.*

17. Realize that happiness can never be found in the mere rearrangement of exterior conditions.

18. *Find yourself reflecting more and more about the inner life.*

19. Prefer quietness to noise.

20. *Glimpse that you cannot be without anything that you really need.*

21. Take no thought for tomorrow because you finally see that you don't need to.

22. *Do not mechanically go along with negative feelings that arise.*

23. See that you get highly paid for working on yourself.

24. *Take as a truth — you have tremendous capacities for happiness which need only day-by-day development.*

## The Opposite Sex and Happiness

"I fall in love with every attractive woman I meet. It's miserable. I meet her and bang, I'm in love. Then the pain begins. I worry that she won't like me, or that I'll lose her. Why does it have to be like this? Why can't love be as nice and romantic as it's supposed to be? This is my secret unhappiness. What can I do?"

"Would you like a frank discussion on this? I may have to tell you things you don't want to hear."

"Please go ahead."

"You have never loved any of these women. You are excited over the pleasure they give you. You feel proud to have an attractive woman at your side, you like the physical affection, or maybe you want sexual relations. You mistake these emotional pleasures for love."

"Maybe you are right. I don't know."

"Notice this. Whenever either of you gets tired of the other, the so-called love flies out the window. Indifference or resentment takes its place."

"Then it wasn't love in the first place. Well, that clarifies at least one thing."

"When you really love another, there is no disturbance whatsoever. The other person can be nice or un-nice, take you or leave you. Your love does not depend upon them behaving the way you want; there are no conditions attached. Whatever happens, you are unaffected and unafraid. Love is a total understanding of yourself in relation to her. Real love has no selfish desire. You love another not because you want something from her, but because it is the very nature of the True Self to love. Don't think all this is sentimentality. This is the answer."

"It is all so original to me. Could you suggest a simple starting point for grasping it?"

"Try to see that love of pleasure from the opposite sex and actually loving her are two entirely different things. Seeing that much, you can now work to understand your own needs for distracting pleasure. Finally, you will never again suffer from this kind of pain. You will be happy with every woman, and every woman on your own level of psychic success will be happy with you."

## Why People Run So Hard

People fail to transform their lives because they don't stick to one rich stream until they catch a glint of gold. They dig here for a minute, then over there, then dash off to the surface glitter of another stream.

How often this happens, when a person tries to understand himself. He sees all his contradictions and frustrations, yet fails to work at understanding them. Take the man who drives himself day and night to achieve fame and fortune. He ruins his health, keeps his family in an uproar, makes himself generally miserable. Obviously, he drives himself because he thinks it gives him something, yet every day ends with the same sense of despair. Why?

It has to do with the imaginary pictures he holds of himself. He identifies himself as a go-getter, a man of achievement, a financial genius or something similar. Having set himself up as being this kind of person, he frantically seeks to bring about exterior results to prove it. But it can *never* be proven, results or not, because this is not his real self at all; it's only an artificial, imaginary, useless mental picture. He can instantly break the mad pattern by dropping all imaginations about himself.

"You don't mean that we should be lazy toward our everyday tasks in business and society?"

"Not at all. I will tell you a secret worth billions of dollars to industry. I am not exaggerating in the slightest when I say billions of dollars. If employers and employees would shed their imaginary pictures of themselves, they would be one hundred percent more efficient at their work. How come? Listen very carefully. Because *imaginary*

161

*self-pictures always induce reactions of despair, depression, carelessness, inefficiency.* You see, a free man is not emotionally entangled with his exterior tasks. He handles his business life with perfect ease and efficiency. Nothing bothers him. His spiritual success makes everything just fine."

"You should tell corporation executives about this!"

"First, their motive must be right. They must want to be free, not to save billions. Remember what we learned about the right order of things? But all this is a deep mystical mystery for you to solve. Spend extra time reflecting on it."

## The Time of Your Life

Discovering the facts about time is like locating a fabulously rich treasure chest. The first fact is that there are two kinds of time: We have man-made time, as measured by clock and calendar. It is useful for handling affairs on the human level, for we need to catch the train on time and we must bake the pie exactly forty minutes.

On the mystical and psychological level, the only time is Now. There are no minutes, days, years, past, or future, only the Eternal Now. This is a vast subject, so we must concentrate our study on seeing how time connects with human happiness.

Make this revealing experiment: The next time you feel unhappy, take a close look. You will detect its link with something that has *already* happened or that you think *will* happen. With most people, the two terrible thieves of happiness are regret of the past, and fear of the future. These thieves operate in the dark, that is, unconsciously. Your Self-Observation exposes them to the light of awareness.

A child on a swing gets scared whenever he swings too far forward or backward. So does torment attack the mind when it needlessly swings into the past or future. When the swing halts at its natural position, we rest quietly.

It is absolutely impossible to be unhappy *Now*. The present moment is perfect freedom, as Alan W. Watts explains:

> ... The letting go or acceptance of your experience and state of mind as it is, is always the act of living completely and perfectly in *this moment*. For we have noted that ego-consciousness is a bondage to time, being essentially a complex of memories and anticipations. All ego-centric action has an eye to the past or the future; in the strict present the ego does not exist. That is easier to prove by experiment rather than by theory, for in concentrating simply and solely upon what is happening at this moment, anticipation and anxiety vanish ... Many masters of the spiritual life have therefore laid especial value upon the exercise of living and thinking simply in this moment, letting the past and future drop out of mind; for the ego drops away with them, together with its pride in the past and its fear and greed for the future.[2]

Spiritual time — or rather, timelessness — connects with every area of life, for example, health. Thousands of patients on sick beds could get up and walk away by penetrating this secret. Psychosomatic illness of every variety springs from the pressure of living in the wrong time.

Don't wander from the safety zone of Now. During your day, observe how your mind slips backward to yesterday and forward to tomorrow. Catch it. Pull it back. Pull it back to where it belongs — in the here and Now.

## How to Change Everything

"I will put the question as simply as I can and would appreciate just as clear and concise an answer as possible. Why don't we see the Reality that could deliver us? Why do we resist our own rescue?"

---

[2] Alan W. Watts, *The Supreme Identity* (London: Faber and Faber, Limited).

"A man cannot see anything he is unwilling to see. He is unwilling because he fears that the loss of his false and fixed viewpoints means the loss of himself. He identifies with these viewpoints; he thinks they are *him*, which they are not. Now, the loss of his old nature is his very rescue, for it leads to Reality, to his True Self. But he will not plunge into the darkness, fearing that there is nothing beyond. There *is*, but every man must take the plunge for himself. Then, everything is different."

Everything is different once we get a glimpse of what our great capacities for happiness are. Ignorance of our true center limits our possibilities, much like a millionaire who cramps himself into one small closet of his fifty-room mansion. We must follow the lead of Heraclitus, the ancient Greek thinker who declared, "I sought for myself."

Everything is different when we are different. Having seen that our conditioned thinking cannot penetrate spiritual heights, we cease trying. Though it is frightening and shattering to the ego-self, we give up, not knowing what will become of us. That does it. The bubble we thought was so beautiful bursts before our eyes, and amazingly, we see beyond it to that which is permanently beautiful.

Our inner transformation now extends itself to everyday affairs, transforming them completely. For example, we now understand that there are two ways of seeing other people, one of them harmful, the other one healthy.

One way we see people: living in a hypnotized state of cruelty, hypocrisy, arrogance, and other negativities. If this viewpoint is an unconscious projection of similar states that exist in us, it is obviously harmful. This means that we unknowingly see others as we are.

There is another way of seeing people in these negative states. We see them as cruel and arrogant, not as an emotionalized projection of our own unseen states, but simply as a fact. It is like seeing a tiger in a zoo. While knowing the tiger is vicious, this knowing is not a projection of our own unconscious cruelty; it is a fact outside ourselves.

Only the man who has freed himself from the tiger within his own system can see the tiger in other people and not be bothered by it.

Whenever we have an unhappy experience with another person, we must not complain, "Why did he do this to me?" That is the first reaction almost everyone makes. However, it misses the mark entirely. Instead you must ask, "Why did I react painfully to what he did?" This reaction brings us back to our responsibility for abandoning ego-centered sensitivities. Then, anyone can do anything to you and there is no pain, only a peaceful understanding.

## The Pleasures of Self-Forgetting

Man's meaningless motions and agonizing appetites are nothing more than attempts to forget himself. Alcohol, social climbing, material acquisition, sexual excess — all are attempts to escape an unwanted self.

What *is* this unwanted self? We come back, as always, to man's false sense of identity. Man yearns to escape from *his own pretensions of who he is.* Inwardly, he knows that he is not the pseudo-self going around with surface smiles, drawing excitement from applause, swelling with pride over some achievement. His intuitive mind tells him that is all an act — and how weary he is of the routine role.

So he tries to forget. But he never succeeds. He always does the wrong thing. His churning and chasing merely cover up the anxiety, leaving it to do its dark destruction.

But there is a genuine way of self-forgetting. The false self and its built-in pains can be demolished. Like a ball of string held at one end and rolled along the floor, the false self can become smaller and smaller and finally disappear

165

altogether. Then you forget it. Who thinks about something that doesn't exist?

All this, of course, is what the Mystic Path is all about. Our goal is to exchange the old life for the new.

How strange. A man is aware that he lives with family and friends, but rarely considers how he lives with himself! The very center is neglected, like keeping the orange peel and tossing away the fruit.

Living with ourselves can be either a very enjoyable experience or a terror, *depending upon which self we live with*. The higher we go, the less we need to think about the personal self. We attain spiritual self-forgetfulness in which we know peace. Our lives are lived for us. We have no worries about what to do, or whether we should do anything, or not. Our day rolls forward with a new and mysterious form of indifference, not of the apathetic kind. This inspiring indifference sees through our pretentious ambitions and frantic strivings. It is passive and yet dynamic, alert, wise. We see more, feel more, live more.

And we don't have to think at all. We are beyond the frustrations of human thought. Rather, we are quietly aware of everything, while being emotionally involved in nothing. We just flow along with a gentle carelessness. What is there to worry about? The worrying self no longer exists!

"There is but one virtue and that is to forget yourself as a person. There is but one vice and that is to think of yourself." (Johann Fichte)

Does this seem strange and remote to you? Listen! Somewhere, deep down, you sense a response. Far below your surface thoughts and feelings, you feel something else quite different, quite thrilling. Do you see it? You will. Do not try to see. Do not think about it. Do nothing. There is nothing you need to do. That is how it goes. It goes all by itself.

## *Lasting happiness in review of this chapter*

1. Try to see what happiness is not. This clears your understanding of what it is.

2. We can be earnest toward life without being grimly serious.

3. A great prize given to the self-liberated man is a new ability for a good time.

4. Self-awakening leads to lasting happiness.

5. Be receptive to inspiring impressions. Let them transform you, quietly and effortlessly.

6. Don't let negative feelings dictate the way you feel.

7. Remember that you now possess all the needed potentialities for happiness in the here and now. Develop them.

8. By understanding the secrets of mystical time, you brighten every hour of your day.

9. The higher you climb in mystical truth, the less you need to bother with yourself.

10. Happiness is a certainty to the man or woman who truly understands it.

# 11

# How to
# Truly Live
# As You Like

People resist any religion or philosophy that seems to limit their everyday pleasures of food, recreation, comfort, sex. Some people think that the higher life is intent on robbing them of the few pleasures they have in life. But any true and *truly beneficial* system does just the opposite. Its purpose is to show people how to enjoy earthly benefits genuinely, while adding the Kingdom of Heaven. Do people *really* enjoy themselves? Not really. They fear the very pleasures they pursue. Food may make them overweight; the party ends at midnight; the lover goes away.

The purpose of a true philosophy is not to take away anything beneficial, but to show people how to enjoy themselves in a newer and more bountiful way.

The object of this book is not merely to supply you with something to read, but rather to *awaken* a *personal witness of Truth within you.* That is the only thing that will ever give security and peace to an insecure and warring world.

Suppose you wandered thirstily about the desert and finally discovered a green oasis from which you drank pure, refreshing water. Going on your way, you met a wanderer whom you told about the oasis. But, instead of believing you, he argued about its existence; he insisted that his scientific calculations proved no oasis could exist in that area. You were undisturbed by his insistence, for after all, you *knew.* Then, another wanderer appeared to profess his independence of your oasis, declaring he had his own. His desperate eyes told you otherwise, but you realized how useless it was to point out his self-deception.

Regardless of the weary wanderers you meet in life; no matter how alarmed, or frightened, or scornful they are, you will retain your quietness. Nothing can shake you. You have personally refreshed yourself from such an oasis. Nothing can ever take away that experience.

We must try to see the difference between *talking about* inner enrichment and the *personal experiencing* of it. Many people, in their unawakened state, blithely think that *talking about* is the same as the experience. What dreadful self-robbery.

But you and I are all through with that. We talked for years and still remained thirsty. We are tired of it. We now want to know the truth from personal witness within. And that is what we can have. We can truly live as we like.

## The Great Search

Every man is making the great search, whether he is consciously aware of it or not. Everything he does, says, thinks, and feels relates to his quest to gain peace, and avoid strife. He busies himself making money, building homes, raising families, attending meetings, all in the hope of winning the prizes.

But, unknowingly, he makes a gigantic blunder. He mistakes emotional-elation for self-happiness. He fails to see the difference between the passing thrill which he gets and the abiding quietude which he seeks. Over the years, his prizes turn out to be empty packages, but, still, he does not awaken to his mistakes.

"I wish I could get over feeling that these ideas are sometimes harsh. What is wrong in having pleasant sensations, like holding hands with the opposite sex?"

"You want to hold the hand of someone of the opposite sex. All right. Nothing wrong with that. But what about your distress when you *don't* have someone's hand to hold? What will you do then? Don't you see that true happiness is not in his or her hand? It is in something far greater; it is in self-freedom, whether or *not* you have the physical and emotional pleasure of a held hand. Try to see what is meant by this."

"I do, in a way. Then it is not harsh after all; I must simply see the whole picture. Fair enough."

"The truth is not really harsh; it only appears that way, because of our ignorance. If you see a careless bird in front of your automobile, you honk the horn, not to scare the bird but to save it."

"How can I make a success of these ideas?"

"Success comes by remembering your purpose of self-release, and forgetting useless distractions. So many people, when they have nothing to do, go ahead and do it anyway."

Become aware of the many false authorities — exterior and interior — seeking to distract you from the great search. Unfortunately, many human beings are like blades of grass, swayed this way and that by every chance breeze of public opinion. They only know what to think after advice is given by someone they assume is wiser than they.

Their feelings for the next hour are determined by the last person with whom they spoke. Whatever happens, they bend in the influenced direction. Worst of all, when nothing happens, they anxiously seek out an external authority — almost always a negative one — for they feel that the worst possible thing that could happen to them is for nothing to happen.

Higher authorities exist. They are Cosmic Principles.

Their cosmic character is so different that you can, with quiet attention, detect their superiority. They are compassionate invitations, not disturbing demands. They want nothing from you; they merely inquire whether you are now ready to receive their gifts.

It is with these inner whisperings, these intuitive influences, that you solve the mystery of existence.

## You Are Unique

Shield yourself from distracting and false authorities by simplifying your efforts. Anything we can do to make things clearer and easier is wise. Over the years, I have worked at reducing profound principles to simple procedures. Let me pass on, for your use, a result of my work. You can call it the *KAB* method, by remembering the first letters in the three steps:

**1.** *K*nowledge

**2.** *A*ction

**3.** *B*rightness

*Knowledge*: Make it your energetic business to find out what you don't know. *Action:* Put your knowledge to work with experimentation, Self-Observation, a willingness to change what must be changed. *Brightness:* Remain cheerful and encouraged by realizing that you can go as far as you want to go.

*KAB* results in what Eastern philosophers call *moksha*, liberation.

Let the principle of repetition help you. Repeatedly read, review, discuss life-giving ideas. But do so alertly, not mechanically. Reading words without grasping their mystical meaning is like examining the menu after being served your dinner.

*Do you understand that cosmic insight alone brings emancipation?*

*Do you see that your aim is to rise above your present self?*

*Do you know that you have a special uniqueness?*

Stop acting as if the other person is unique and you are commonplace. That is idol worship which produces pain. Act as if you are unique, not from human vanity, but because it is so. You are unique. To really see it, we must first extinguish counterfeit uniqueness based on egotistical imaginations of our own goodness. As the human self fades, the True Self appears. That is what is unique about you and me. And we had better start living that uniqueness.

Even if you do not understand a principle relating to the better life, you need not go on to misunderstanding it. Leave the mind at rest, thus making room for eventual comprehension.

Be patient. If you simply let things come in their own natural way you can handle them with natural intelligence. It is our unnatural forcing of life that causes grief. We cannot hasten tomorrow by ripping a page off the calendar. Neither need we be concerned with our mystic progress. It needs no force. Eventually, you will let each day dawn spontaneously with the realization that it is right because you are right.

Seneca, a mystic who served as Prime Minister to Emperor Nero, showed clear insight by remarking that men are happy when "beyond the influence of fear and desire."

## How to Stay Out of Trouble

No man in constant trouble lives as he likes. So to live truly as we like we need plans for keeping free of trouble. There are such plans. By trouble I mean both exterior difficulties and the disturbances churning around our minds and feelings. People head straight for trouble, like a runaway automobile, because they do not pay attention to these plans — which are higher truths.

When a higher truth finally sinks into mind and heart, you never again suffer the penalty for not knowing that truth. You enjoy its radiating health permanently. Examples:

*By seeing the real meaning of life in inner advancement, we destroy painful feelings of futility.*

*By refusing to limit ourselves, we expand far beyond our fondest dreams.*

*By awareness of whatever may be false in us, we permit revelation of all that is true.*

*By letting love be the perfect guide, we walk lightly.*

*By union with our true nature, we never again suffer from a divided self.*

*By realizing the limitations of thought-power, we attain the greater power of conscious awareness.*

*By being receptive to positive impressions only, we refresh ourselves minute by minute.*

What kind of impression are you making on yourself? It is self-enriching to find out.

Every twenty-four hours you receive thousands of positive and negative impressions. They come from outside and within. You see a glittering lake, or you overhear a gloomy remark, or someone smiles at you — and you have three separate impressions. You silently recall an incident from yesterday, or wonder about tomorrow's weather — and have two more impressions.

Impressions flow in a constant stream; you need do nothing to invite them, and you cannot stop them. *But the kind of impressions admitted to your mind make your life what it is.*

Upon reaching a certain level of psychic awareness you have the power to receive only healthy impressions, the cheery and helpful ones. If negative impressions come your way, you will be able to stop them before they penetrate to make you sad or upset. Unhealthy impressions are like thieves in the night, who steal your psychic riches, leaving you poor and exhausted. You cannot stop them from trying to enter, but you can prevent them from actually penetrating. By becoming aware of them, by exposing the thieves in the night, you destroy them. It is as if you have the magic ability to dissolve a flying stone before it strikes you.

There are millions of beautiful impressions, and they are all for you. There are enough to make you a supremely happy man or woman. You need only exclude the unwanted impressions and welcome the happy ones.

## How to Live As You Like with Others

If we think that other people can do us good, we will also think the opposite, that they can do us harm. It is an esoteric principle that neither is true. It is a subtle form of idol worship to think that anyone of himself does anything good or bad for us. However, others can be channels for our good.

Genuine fulfillment arises from within yourself. To feel alive only when we are with another person is false vitality, which we fear losing with the loss of the other. By extinguishing that part of us which feels alive only when with another is to live truly.

I want to give you a profound principle which, when absorbed, enables you to live as you like with other people.

You cannot establish a solid and satisfying relationship with another through human devices, such as gifts,

174

promises, persuasions, threats, flatteries. You might temporarily get what you want, but the relationship will not be a happy one, and it will most likely break up.

Satisfying relationships can exist only between people who are more or less on the same high level of psychic maturity. They can enjoyably exchange endless benefits with each other on the psychic level, such as love and understanding. They can also, without tension, enjoy all the benefits of the human and physical level, like conversation, companionship, sex. But two people on a low level of maturity can only anxiously exchange gifts on the human level, for that is all they have.

This leads us right back to the same conclusion: Raise your own level of psychic understanding, of mental maturity. Then you automatically attract people on your new level and with them you can have happy relations.

Picture yourself standing opposite someone with circles drawn on the floor around each of you. The two circles represent psychological zones of influence, his and yours. Now, when meeting another person, do not enter his zone of influence. This means that you do not abandon your mind and emotions to him; it means that you are unafraid of him. Stay within your own circle of self-influence. You then maintain your integrity and command the situation.

This does not mean that you dominate the other person in the usual meaning of the word; it means you are in perfect command, because you have no need to dominate. Here is a mystical mystery for you to ponder and solve: The greatest power on earth is no power at all.

Flatly refuse to let anyone put pressure on you. In some cases this means a calm but firm statement that he or she must stop it. When done correctly it is a favor to both of you. A bully might resent being told to "knock it off," but at the same time he will like you, for he is secretly glad to find someone who isn't bluffed by his childish pressure.

In other circumstances, perhaps in a husband and wife

situation, where it is best not to speak up at the moment, you must refuse inwardly. This must not be done in anger, but in silent understanding of why the other person behaves so badly. The world is thick with tactless and overbearing people. We must, therefore, keep ready our inward refusal. Let no pressuring person make you feel pressured. You have the power to remain perfectly calm in every difficult and unexpected event in life.

## What to Do with Your Day

"I feel that my life is in the hands of other people. It makes me uncomfortable to realize that my peace is at the mercy of their changeable moods."

"No person has power to either give you happiness or take it away."

"Then how come I feel good with some people?"

"Because you confuse happiness with pleasurable sensations. They are entirely different. Happiness is purely an inner state, unrelated to other people; therefore, they can neither give happiness, nor withdraw it. Think of someone you were madly in love with a few years ago. That person is the same; *you* feel differently."

"But I still feel good with some people."

"Yes, but try to see that this good feeling is not the same thing as enduring happiness. It is a sensation which *is* at the mercy of changeable people. Do you really think that life is so unfair as to place your well-being into the hands of fickle people? Sensations come and go; happiness endures."

"But I want to enjoy people."

"You will enjoy them in a new way, once you see the truth about this. You now have a painful fear of losing the pleasurable sensations derived from others. That will disappear; you won't be afraid to lose anyone from your life."

"You have awakened something I never sensed before."

"Remember that real happiness never changes; regardless of exterior conditions, it just *is*."

Happiness is a state of psychic understanding, not of emotional feeling. We must understand who we really are, and why we act as we do. With that understanding, we can safely let glad feelings arise as they will. Such feelings are legitimate; there is no swing of the pendulum back to gloom. When you attend a lively party, do not try to take happiness from the people and the distractions. Happiness does not exist in those things — and you sense it, don't you? Go to the party in a state of self-awareness, and you will enjoy it like no one else in the room. Unlike the others, your enjoyment will remain with you after the ball is over.

In Balzac's mystical novel, *Louis Lambert*, the question arises as to why we are here on earth. Answer: Because we have interior themes to develop and enjoy. So you see, you have much better things to do with your day than waste it in not living as you like.

## Four Steps to New Harmony

You must never consent to a human relationship based in fear. This does not mean that you necessarily end the relationship, but you end the fear in it. Take these four steps:

**1.** Think of someone whom you fear in one way or another. (You must honestly admit the fear; otherwise, nothing can be done.) Select someone with whom you are in frequent contact. You will employ this relationship in building new courage toward everyone.

**2.** Act and think and speak toward this person in the way that *you* desire. Do not mentally submit to him or her. Crack your usual behavior pattern. Dare to risk offending him with your new independence. It is absolutely necessary that you dare risk offending him. You are afraid because you don't want him to get mad at you. *Risk it; let him get mad if he wants to*. But assert yourself in very

177

small ways at first. If you take too much at one time you won't be able to make yourself do it.

**3.** As you act up, keep yourself emotionally uninvolved with whatever happens. Stand aside and observe the reactions and results, both within yourself and in the situation. Watch whatever occurs with an air of indifference to consequences.

**4.** Persistent practice will give you a new sense of independence, which, incidentally, you had all along but didn't realize. Now, with awareness of your natural freedom, you can enjoy it. And you won't be afraid of any other human being on the face of the earth.

As you do all this, you will observe a definite change in your attitudes and actions toward others. You are *genuinely* independent. You are not afraid of offending them as you used to be. You are free of the awfully anxious thought that they might leave you or not like you any more. You command them in an entirely new way, through no command whatsoever. You let them behave as they wish, while you keep your peace whatever their behavior. To be free of other people — that is the goal. And that is authentic compassion, for freedom from others provides the psychic ability to love them.

We have great capacity for harmony, which we can deliberately develop far beyond our present position. We must not carelessly limit ourselves to what we already have. We must not take the limit of our view as the limit of our capacity. Whenever you ask, "Can even this be transformed?" the answer is always, "Yes, even this." As an example, we can review a previous point: By living out the principles of the Mystic Path today, we free ourselves of the consequences of wrong human relationships of yesterday.

## An Act of Genuine Compassion

Your happiness with others does not depend upon what they think of you. That is slavery and painful tension. "Moreover, consider what your bondage is in the world. What do you suffer to keep the esteem of men you dislike?" (Francois Fénelon)

Your happiness depends upon what you think of yourself. That is freedom and relaxation. To place your well-being in the hands of another is like wanting a painting of a colorful dawn, but meekly allowing the artist to paint what he prefers, perhaps a bowl of fruit. You must stop that. Even if it produces a temporary emotional crisis in you — which it will — you must stop it. You must please yourself as your inner integrity tells you to do, regardless of consequences. You must consent to nothing that compromises with what you know is right for you. And that inner voice is always telling you what is right, isn't it?

"I am annoyed by the shallow and often senseless behavior of friends and relatives. You say that the problem is my annoyance, not their behavior. I'd like to dismiss my negative reactions, but how?"

"Don't believe that they can do any better than they do. A child of five can't behave like a child of ten. The same with adults. No one can possibly behave above his own level of understanding. Don't expect people to do any better than they are compelled to do at their present level. Your problem is in assuming that they should and could behave better. That is like thinking that a monkey should be as dignified as a deer. Understand this and annoyance disappears."

"I get upset and confused when the people in my life get into trouble. I want to help but don't know how. What is my responsibility?"

"You must never take responsibility for another's mistake. And you must never sentimentally excuse it, any more than you excuse your own mistakes. A false sense of love or loyalty on our part robs the other person of the learning process. Even if the other person refuses to learn the lesson, that is his responsibility. This may seem harsh, but it is an act of compassion. Even Christ refused to take responsibility for those who refused his message."

As you gradually awaken to mystical enlightenment, you will feel the urge to share your discovery with others. It is good and natural for you to pass along what the New Testament refers to as a pearl of great price. Because you will find others in various stages of receptivity, remember this: Never give more than others can understand and appreciate at the moment. This is cosmic law. To try to give what others cannot receive is like tossing a ball against a brick wall — it bounces back to strike you. Jesus explained this law by saying that we should not cast our pearls before swine; that is, before those whose incomprehension of truth makes them indifferent or hostile to it.

But some will be eager to know more. With such receptive people you will establish a radiant relationship unlike anything else on earth. You help each other to truly live as you like.

## When You Don't Know What to Do

"What questions are asked most often by seekers?"

"People ask how to be free, how to work on themselves. People want to know how to proceed."

"And the answer?"

"There are many excellent techniques. An individual can choose those best suited to his own taste. It is like a dozen upward trails winding up to the top of a mountain. A climber can start anywhere at the base of the mountain and hike upward."

"Please supply examples of profitable techniques."

"Observe yourself with the intention of seeing yourself as you actually are, not as you imagine you are. Read books by authors who have found the way themselves. Constantly realize that nothing stands in your way but your own conditioned mind. Get tired and more tired of not living your own life. Dare to think in new ways. There are hundreds of helpful techniques. Channel them into your single aim — self-insight which provides self-freedom."

"According to the Mystic Path, what is positive action?"

"Whatever is done consciously, with awareness, is positive action. Inner enlightenment is genuine action. Suppose a businessman likes to picture himself as highly competent. He may be competent in financial matters, but a family crisis leaves him confused. It is positive action for him to see that business skill cannot be transferred to family affairs. Seeing his weakness, being aware of it, his self-study can now add new profit."

"Then it is positive to notice negativities within ourselves, like weakness and guilt?"

"Of course. Nothing is more positive. Never forget — awareness of a negativity is the cure, the *only* cure of the negativity."

"But we don't like to see the dark side of ourselves."

"No, because you still identify with them. You take them as being *you*, which they are not. Observe the dark features, but do not say "I" to them. This is a gigantic secret which you must explore thoroughly. The time will come when you can observe anger or anguish within you as being entirely separate from your natural self. You are then beautifully free."

When you do not know what to do, you have no responsibility to do anything, except to be aware that you are lost. Do not do anything but that. Do not permit nervous anxiety to drive you to futile exterior activities. You are not shirking rightful responsibility when you refrain like this; you are wisely avoiding the consequences of muddled action. Clarity, clarity, clarity; our first duty is to think clearly. Make it your rule to understand things, which you can surely do. Then, your action will be right.

The most trivial act becomes dynamic when you attempt it with self-awareness. Whether you are washing dishes, or painting a table, or simply walking from one room to another, try to be aware of yourself doing just that. Don't just paint or walk, but be conscious of yourself painting or walking. This detaches you from the dream state in which most people live; it puts you in touch with your energetic center self. Any action performed with self-awareness becomes inspired.

## You Can Start The Great Change

How do you learn to live as you like? There is nothing at all complicated about it. You start. You start living as you like. And you can do that by ceasing to involve yourself with activities and people you don't really enjoy. You know what they are. Your deeper self tells you of the things you do from a false sense of duty, from false loyalty, from public pressure, from trying to please unpleasant people so that they will be pleased with you.

*Learn to live as you like by no longer living as you dislike.*

But you must rebel against your own mental chains and nothing else. You will miss it entirely if you become a social reformer, or if you strike against people whom you think are keeping you down. No offensive individual and no social silliness can keep you down. We are responsible for our own chains, and we are capable of our own liberation.

"I resist some of these ideas because I feel they may take away things I don't want to give up."

"Like what?"

"Like living my own life as I see fit."

"*Are* you living your own life?"

"I suppose."

"Does it make you happy?"

"Well, not really."

"Then are you truly living as you like, or are you unconsciously enslaved by false ideas of what it means to live your own life — ideas, incidentally, imposed upon you by a confused society? When you really live as you like you are genuinely happy."

"That makes sense."

"Empty your mind of the belief that you already know what it means to live as you like. Don't be afraid of the emptiness; there is nothing to fear. Remain with it, and one day, it will be filled with an amazing revelation."

Suppose a law were passed denying us the right to speak or write any words containing the first ten letters of the alphabet. Such a law would produce frustration and nervous tension. Because it would be unnatural and unnecessary, it could not be obeyed, even by those who sincerely tried.

Likewise, all negativities are unnatural and unnecessary to us. People live tensely frustrated lives, because they wrongly assume they are subject to prohibitive laws. There are no prohibitions to liberty; there is only a false belief in them.

A man is a problem to himself, because he does not live from the facts of life. This could be remedied all right, except for another problem: A man will not persistently shove aside his illusions which he thinks are facts in favor of facts which he thinks are illusions. But he can reverse things; he can change. Goethe, the German poet and dramatist, showed sharp insight into this when he wrote, "Man seeks his inward unity, but his real progress on the path depends upon his capacity to refrain from distorting reality in accordance with his desires."

To start the great change you must rise up and declare with all the power within you, "I have lived this frustrating way all my life, but regardless of what now happens to me, I flatly refuse to live that way any longer." You may do this with fear and trembling, but, never mind, just do it.

Yes, *that* pressure too. *That* can also go. I mean the one you have about your finances. You want to know whether there is a way to get by financially without being a slave to the time clock and to the dread of another wasted day, doing what you don't want to do. Yes, that can go too. You can truly live as you like.

## *Special points to remember in this chapter*

1. You can truly live as you like.

2. Let Cosmic Principles guide your great search. They never fail.

3. You find your genuine uniqueness by working patiently with the ideas of the Mystic Path.

4. We remain free of trouble when we learn to receive positive impressions only.

5. There is a right way and a wrong way to live with others. You are now studying the right way.

6. We have better things to do with our day than waste it in undesirable states of mind.

7. Do not mentally consent to a human relationship based in fear.

8. Please yourself as your own integrity directs.

9. As self-awareness grows, you become more skilled in human relations. Everything brightens.

10. Start the great change today. Live as you truly like.

# 12

## How to Be
## an Entirely
## New Person

Whenever you hear religious or philosophical ideas, ask yourself, "Do they helpfully relate to my everyday life of getting along with people, with my inner turmoils, with my concern over events?" If the ideas are meaningless words, words, words, you are wasting energy that should be spent in *connecting cosmic truths with your everyday life*. This lets you be in the very center of life's turmoil and yet be completely unaffected. Challenge every idea offered you with, "Will it lead to self-transformation?"

Suppose a group of explorers want to reach the peak of a great mountain. But as they sit around camp, they begin arguments. One man accuses another of not getting a proper haircut. Two more disagree over whether the animal they saw was a rabbit or squirrel. A third couple sit and glare at each other without knowing why.

That is exactly what the mass of men do. They argue over theology, psychic phenomena, over words and slogans and personalities, over laws and social reforms — all the while thinking that they are perfectly intelligent, reasonable men, going somewhere. They go nowhere, for as Emerson observes, "Society never advances. It recedes as fast on one side as it gains on the other." The best evidence that the mass of men never get anywhere is seen in the frightened look that comes to the eyes of people in off-guard moments.

If a truly wise man happened to be nearby those explorers, he would shout, "Stop all that foolishness. Climb!"

Not all would hear him, but perhaps a man or two would sense the message. He would see the futility of words and the need for personal action. He would decide to break away to become a true individualist. He would climb. And he would reach the peak.

That is where you come in. But first you must want to be a genuinely new person more than you want anything else, more than *anything*. That leads to inspired action. Then you can climb, and with resolute persistence, you will stand above the world.

Use this method for making the most of your studies: Whenever you meet a striking idea, do not assume that you understand it fully. This common tendency must be avoided. Rather, assume that you barely glimpse its glitter. An explorer who comes upon a magnificent, long-lost temple in the wilderness does not believe that his first glance includes the whole structure. No, he explores persistently and eagerly, room by room, treasure by treasure.

Perhaps an idea in this book awakens your intuition. Make a note of its location. Review it once a day for several days. Do not read dutifully, just to get it done, but with love for discovery. Have the joyful curiosity of the psychic scientist, which you are. Try to connect it with other principles. See its deeper meaning. Ask how it can benefit you in practical ways. It is safe to say that every new idea contains a thousand times the treasure we first suspect. Let us get on to it.

But, with all your studies, remember this: One minute of experiencing the free flow of life for yourself is worth a thousand hours with books and lectures. You don't want to read the menu; you want to taste the dinner. Knowledge is needed, yes, but let it be the gateway to spaciousness.

## The Magic Power of Wonderment

A man or woman painfully explains, "You know, in spite of all my busy activities, I really don't know what to do with myself. Oh, I have my television and social life; I don't mean things like that. I mean my inner self. It's all so empty and pointless. Yes, that's the whole problem; I just don't know what to do about my inner emptiness. It aches so badly."

Of course it does. Such a confession by one man or woman is an honest reflection shared by millions of trapped people. They just don't know what to do with themselves. Their secret emptiness makes every day a new terror. They desperately hope to find enough artificial activities to get them through another empty day.

You need not live that way. There is a new way. Take courage and know it can be yours. I will give you a technique that can be used with magical effect, if you will but work with it: The very next time you feel overwhelmed by confusion or emptiness, look at this psychic state with a sense of wonderment, yes, wonderment. Don't react with customary fright or resistance. Calmly sit down and try to see what it is all about. Be cheerfully curious, just as if it is a new adventure in self-discovery, for that is just what it is.

Something quite remarkable will happen before your

eyes. You will see this state in an amazing new way. It will no longer be emptiness, but something else, something which I cannot describe to you, but which you can know for yourself. The darkness turns to light.

The next time you do not know what to do with your emptiness, look at it with a sense of wonderment.

Your resolve to change yourself will certainly arouse protests from your deeply-entrenched habits, but you must flatly refuse to listen. Ignore their accusations. Stay with yourself. And especially — don't fear the consequences of breaking free.

We must recognize this subtle enemy called fear of consequences. Unless we are alertly aware of its terrible tyranny, it keeps us its unconscious slave. By consequences, I mean whatever happens to you — inwardly or outwardly — as a result of your blow for personal liberty.

Do not fear consequences from anyone, or anything. Do what you must do and quietly observe what happens. Stand up in the face of reactions from other people, or from your own negative nature. You broke away from that relationship because you can no longer live that kind of life? You acted heroically. You refused to compromise yourself by agreeing with someone simply because you value his friendship? Good. You dared to look within yourself and were shocked to see more negativity than you suspected? That is a positive act.

Whatever the consequences, even if painful, let them teach you the lesson. They are trying to tell you of another way to live. They do their best to break you free of the monotonous life.

*Whatever happens*, start each new day with wonderment, as if it were the very first day of your life. This should be done by anyone who doesn't want his future to be repetition of his past.

189

## Something You Must Realize

One psychic fact cannot be repeated too often: We will never break free to newness until we get utterly tired of old bondage. But to get tired of it, we must first become conscious that we *are* slaves to a thousand and one things. We must see it deeply, even painfully, not superficially. We must be weary of worrying over finances; we must get fed up with being scared and lonely. Yes, we must get horrified at the tragedy of our life. This conscious facing of our emptiness makes us tired of living that way any longer. Now, we are getting smart.

Never ask, "What is the alternative to my present way? What will I have in its place?" To do so is to fall into a trap. To ask these questions prompts the conditioned mind to project what you *desire* this state to be in order to feel secure. Then, anything resembling that state will be mistakenly taken as newness, which it is not. It is merely another chair on the same floor of the building; it is not a higher level of the building.

Have the trust neither to know nor care about your future. Your task is to leave the past. Do that much and your future will unfold in a new way.

Know that you are free right now, for that is a fact. Realize that the real self can behave as if it feared nothing, for it is simply so. Understand that you need not submit yourself to anyone on earth, for a dignified uprightness is your present possession. Recognize that tomorrow is already just fine, for this pre-recognition is accurate. Be aware that nothing can bar you from the abundant life, for abundance is meant for you.

Such truths often puzzle people. They ask, "But how can I know that I am free, when I feel I am not? How can I say something that seems so untrue?" That is a superb question, for it indicates an honest probing of a puzzlement.

It is like sitting at the window of a train passing through a darkly dangerous jungle. You look out to see all sorts of fierce beasts. If your imagination runs wild and you fail to realize that you are on a safe train, you will be scared and nervous. We must be constantly aware of where we really are. We are on the spiritual train that carries us safely past the seeming threats of the exterior world. With that consciousness, we can serenely sit back to enjoy the trip.

Freedom is your actual state at this very instant. You need only realize it with spiritual discernment. By doing this, you have liberty and strength unknown by those who are considered great in public eyes. They know nothing of this secret force, nor do they want it, for it means the end of their ego-centered life. To live from egotism is minute-by-minute slavery, as every slave knows.

You will be great in a different way. You will be carried through every day with no worries and no hurts. You will personally know what every religious teacher has been trying to tell mankind throughout the ages. You will feel the personal miracle of self-transformation.

## How to Walk Away from Problems

Imagine yourself captured by a wicked magician who wishes to use you as a slave around his dreary manor. Knowing you will not consciously consent, he slips you a potion creating the illusion that you cannot escape from the grounds. But the fact is, the manor has neither walls nor guards; you are perfectly free to walk away any time you choose.

Now, what is your problem? To hammer painfully against the walls? What walls? To battle the guards? They don't exist. No, the problem is not to *do* something, but to *see* something. Seeing is the only effective doing. You are not walled in by either a trivial problem, or by the most serious crisis you can imagine. You are free right now, at the very instant you read this line. See it.

I wish that, as seekers of Bliss, which all of us are, you would try to experience for yourselves that universal

191

truth which is in all and may be felt by all. This state is not an invention of anyone. It is already there. We have simply to discover it.[1]

An intellectual examination of a truth does not free us inwardly. We may start with mental examination, but must dare to go beyond it to higher perception, for that alone brings about the New Birth urged by the New Testament. The great danger to a seeker is his careless assumption that intellectual activity is the same as spiritual awareness. It is no more the same than examining a grounded airplane and thinking that it is the same as flying high.

We must pass from thinking our life to living it. A classic book of mysticism, *Theologia Germanica*, confirms, "... we are speaking of a certain Truth which it is possible to know by experience."

It is as if a polar bear tried to explain to his cub what it feels like to swim in the sea. The cub, being able to think only in terms of his present environment on land, could not possibly translate his parent's words into meaning. But as he plunges into the sea for himself, he knows.

Remember: A truth that a man does not understand does not exist for him. Even though giving lip-service, such as publicly declaring that inner values are all that count, he will secretly disbelieve or even scorn it. And since he cannot see this truth, he cannot be paid by it. Understanding is everything.

When a truth is actually understood, it changes us. It is so incredibly different from what we had imagined that we meet the surprise of our lives. It is wonderment, relief, exaltation.

Be willing to receive higher instruction from those who know — the genuine mystics. There are thousands of people who cannot help you; only a few who can. Listen to *them*. It takes a lighted candle to light another.

[1] Paramahansa Yogananda, *The Science of Religion* (Los Angeles: Self-Realization Fellowship, 1953).

## The Self-Confidence of a New Man

I said before that this book is for those who want to escape. One reason for escape is the battering influences of everyday life. Most people are left dizzy and exhausted by the rainstorm of people and events.

I give you assurance: All can be altered. The only necessary and healthy influences are those arising within your original nature. They are the only kind of influences that need affect you.

I give you assurance: The Truth within is stronger than your fears, a person who dislikes you, your boss at work, restlessness, shattered hopes, scary headlines, someone who seems to dominate and threaten you, the accusations of failure and defeat from your own mind, illness, social hypocrisy, a demanding government, enslaving habits, boredom, panic over the future, depression, a sense of ruin, heartache, fear of God, aloneness and loneliness, anxiety over loss of something valuable, collapse of your strength, the terrifying suspicion that life is passing you by, a nagging business complication, humiliation, utter confusion as to what to do and how to do it. The Truth, which is always a part of you, is always stronger than anything else.

When a single idea like this is permitted its dynamic entrance, it vibrates your whole psychic system with new power, just as a single beat vibrates the whole drum. If you will study, review, reflect until you catch even a first glimpse of its mystical meaning, you will make more progress in that time than perhaps in all previous years. The incoming idea magically turns into personal meaning.

All welcomed ideas change into personal meaning when we dare to seek first the Kingdom of Heaven. Please do not react to this as a mere religious truth you have heard before. It is that, all right, but taking it as a nice but impractical church concept will do nothing for you. Take it as being as practical as apple pie. It is as useful to you as that.

One exciting benefit provided by your newness is an amazing self-confidence that you never before thought possible. You laugh at things that used to bother you. You do, and say, and think things that would have horrified you before; but now you know they are right, just fine and right. A psychologist like William James would say you are disinhibited. A philosopher like Epictetus would remark that you have found yourself at last. An Eastern teacher like Chuang-tse would observe that you have, thank heaven, cut the nonsense from your mind to live as nature intended.

But call it what you like, you are fearless. You cheerfully risk everything, because you know you have nothing to lose. You no longer care what others think. You used to be timid, because you thought they could harm or benefit you; but now you know better — your good is from a single Supreme Source. You are a bird set free from the cage of human power.

You daringly defy the world and win every time. But it is a quiet daring, having nothing of the egotism of the old nature. It is humble. Having lost your false sense of self — that egotistical sense of self that causes all griefs — you have the new humility of the True Self. You are actually a *new person*. And how merrily you roll along!

## Where Do You Stand?

I want to talk with you for a few minutes about a subject of supreme significance. I start by asking a question: Can you imagine what it would be like if you had no ideas at all about your spiritual life? Can you conceive it? What if you had no attitudes and beliefs whatsoever about yourself in relation to God, deliverance, eternity, and other spiritual matters? Examine your mind for a moment and you will unearth hundreds of fixed ideas about these subjects.

Suppose, just suppose, you had none of them. In this

vacant state, who would you be? How would you identify yourself? You would not be the kind of person you now take yourself as being at all. That is so, is it not?

Perhaps you say, "But, if I had no attitudes, I would have no foundation from which to think. I would be empty, feel myself as nothing." Yes, you are getting the point. In this state of nothingness, you could not possibly say, "I am a spiritual person, I am sincere, I know what I am talking about when it comes to religious matters." Your emptiness would make you consciously disturbed by tearing away all seeming securities. You would plainly see how frightened you are.

To repeat the question, what if you knew nothing, had no assurances, were completely adrift without your present mental anchors?

*In that seemingly helpless state you would be an entirely different kind of person than you now are.* Is that not a fact?

It is really quite simple. Your life is now what it is because you *do* think from your present ideas. You would not live the same way if you did not have them.

Now let me ask a second question: Your presently possessed attitudes — what *kind* of a life have they given you up to now? You must answer this to yourself with every ounce of frankness within you. Have they supplied the peace you wish, the freedom of spirit in which there is no secret despair, no unspoken dread, and no suppressed shakiness? What is your answer?

We are examining something so immense that it is beyond the power of words to convey. But it is fully within the power of your True Self to comprehend.

I did not ask whether your ideas have given you a busy day, or social success, or financial security. Only this: Have they supplied that Secret Something which you seek, in the utmost depths of your being, with a yearning far greater than you can possibly express?

Now, what if you voluntarily and casually dropped every belief that makes you the kind of person you are?

I wonder whether you will make the voluntary choice to do just this? I invite you to do so. Do not think it is a threat to you. It is not. It is deliverance. It is no threat to *you*, the essential you. It is a threat, be glad, to everything false and frightening. That is what you really want: the destruction of false foundations, cleverly disguised, that only *appear* to support.

It is as if you were standing on a shaky platform watching a passing parade. While one part of your mind tries to enjoy the show, another part trembles with the shakiness beneath your feet. You sense the need to abandon the false structure, but hesitate for fear it will rob you of the passing show. It would not, of course, but because you know of nothing but that insecure platform, you are paralyzed in place.

What is beneath the platform? Solid ground. Even if you are unaware of it as yet, there is solid ground upon which there can be no nervous tension. By standing upon it, you would have no responsibility, no need to do anything but relax and enjoy whatever comes along.

I do not want to go deeper into this astonishing idea for now, not in this book. I want to leave with you just this much to think about: Where would you stand if every false platform, every wrong impression imposed upon you since birth, were removed? What if you no longer stood upon them? In that case, where would you stand?

## If You Feel You Are Missing Out

One of the most powerful of all motivating forces in man is that he not miss out on something. We don't want life to pass us by. Properly directed, this force can turn a poor pilgrim into a wealthy resident. The non-enlightened man *is* missing out; oh, what he is missing, if only he could see it! A man must begin to suspect that there is something else within himself, something entirely different from what he now experiences.

"You speak often of the need for self-transformation. I know this has nothing to do with exterior religious activities, but with inner change. How can I begin?"

"By living from all these new principles that we discuss. This includes self-awareness, ceasing to waste energy in worry and guilt, being receptive to the inner voice, and so on."

"How does this differ from the way the average man lives?"

"The average person lives from old, fixed, negative ideas. He is unaware that he is mechanically driven by frantic desires and habitual responses to life's challenges. It is a strangely tragic situation. For years you can tell a man that he is mechanical, conditioned, unfree, unhappy, and he will never believe you. He has so blocked his mind from seeing himself as he really is that he refuses to see his own chains."

"Then how does anyone ever break free?"

"With most people it takes a severe shock of some kind. An intense suffering often makes them seek the light. Correctly used, shock and suffering can be the turning point toward a new life. But it must be correctly used, that is, constructively."

"Interesting. You say that an awareness of how unhappy we really are can start us toward genuine happiness?"

"Yes. It is not negative to admit we have lost our way; it is an honest step in the right direction. Remember the parable of the Prodigal Son."

It is never your responsibility to *create* success. Your part is to make an effort to awaken to your True Self, whose very nature is success. You need only let it exist in your awakened consciousness.

We must wake up. Fine. But how?

We can take our answer from a thinker who was more or less ignored by the world of his day, but who has since been acclaimed as a mystic of profound insight. Danish author, Soren Kierkegaard, would declare:

"You are in utter despair about yourself? Good. That is a needed step toward liberation. But you must face your despair fully and deeply, and not lull yourself to sleep with comforting doctrines, or shallow escapes. Face the fact of being what you are, for that is what changes what you are. Far from being your shame and ruin, honest Self-Observation leads to the very salvation for which you would gladly give everything."

A city once built an expensive highway that went nowhere. It left the city, twisted around the countryside for a bit, and ended abruptly. A motorist, expecting to reach a definite destination, wasted his time and energy. So do we waste ourselves, when traveling through life on false principles. We must learn to separate the true from the false. The preceding paragraph contains a true principle.

Can you think of anything more exciting than to feel that you are on the right road at last?

## A Life-Transforming Secret

If you will give special attention to the ideas of this section until you grasp them fully, I assure you that your life will be utterly transformed. You are about to explore one of the great esoteric secrets of the ages.

*Men are desperate, and frustrated, and frightened because they live from imaginary pictures they have of themselves, rather than from their true nature.*

If you spent a dozen years working to grasp that single fact, it would not be too much. It is that vital to you. Once more:

Men are desperate, and frustrated, and frightened because they live from imaginary pictures they have of themselves, rather than from their true nature.

198

## How to Be an Entirely New Person

A man must observe that he *is* living from imaginary pictures of who he is, from a false sense of identity. At the start, it is difficult to do this because he is so close to himself that he cannot see his fictitious selves.

For example, suppose a man has been conditioned since childhood with the idea that he must become a great financial success. He begins to see himself as scoring great financial triumphs, buying and selling famous hotels, traveling around the world in luxury, and so on. But when his dream-picture clashes with reality, when he finds himself working in the office, he feels frustrated from the clash between what he is and what he falsely thinks he should be. He should be nothing but a harmonious, cheery, decent human being, either with money or flat broke. By seeing this he would be the happiest office man on earth.

There are endless varieties of artificial selves, but all are equally harmful. People imagine they must be wealthy, popular, wise, lively, educated, powerful, impressive, charming, clever. They must be nothing of the sort. They must be themselves. Then, all the extras of life that we need will be added to us. We will enjoy them, not be possessed by them.

Imaginary self-pictures also explain mankind's wars and crimes and other social tragedies. People, dominated by false ideas of who they are, will be compulsively driven to greed and destructive ambition. When you see that millions of people are hounded by their false identities, you will understand why the world is so wounded.

The destruction of the false self is a great esoteric secret that few of the billions on earth know about. Of those who have heard, few follow it through to self-liberation. You can, if you choose, be different from billions of desperate people. You can work with this idea until it becomes part of your understanding. And then you will live as a new person.

What can you do? You can observe yourself daily.

Watch your daydreams. They are clues to false pictures you have of whom you think you *should* be. Never mind who you *should* be. That is a painful trap. Destroy your imaginary self-pictures with ruthless persistence. They are foes who prevent your newness.

We resist letting go of our imaginary self-pictures because we fear our emptiness without them. We must courageously face the temporary uncertainty as to who we are, if we are to discover our true spiritual identity. All the great religions, including that of the New Testament, tell about this stage of our development. It is like continuing through a dark tunnel to reach finally the sunlight beyond.

## You Can Choose Newness

You have nothing to *do*. You have everything to *be*. People are so confused about what to do with their family affairs, love life, finances, health. And no matter what they do, nothing helps very much. Of course it doesn't. Nothing can be truly different until the individual is different, *really different internally*. *Doing* without *being* is a dreadful way to spend the day, as millions know. But you can be different.

Suppose a man without musical training were to sit before a piano day after day and try to produce enjoyable music. No matter what he did, regardless of how hard he tried, nothing but discord came out. If he occasionally struck a harmonious chord it was purely accidental and was soon lost in the next noise.

Suppose he grew tired of discord and made up his mind to understand its cause. He consults a teacher of piano:

"I don't understand why I can't play the piano."

"Very simple. You must change yourself."

"In what way?"

"You have to understand the principles of music."

"But I already do."

"No. This is your whole problem. You insist that you

already know. But you don't. If you really understood, you would play harmoniously. It is as simple as that."

"So what do I do?"

"Stop trying to *do* things with that piano. It will get you nowhere, as you have already proved. Instead, *be* someone. Be someone who understands the principles of music. Then, you have no problem in *doing*. It will be easy, accurate, enjoyable, rewarding."

That illustrates how millions of people fail to produce daily harmony. Even when something goes well for awhile, they fear future discord. They know it will come, because it always does.

But it need not come any more. I assure you that it can be a thing of the past; gone forever. We need only make a sincere effort to be someone who understands the principles of life. They are available to anyone who really wants them.

People say to me, "I think I have power to transform my life, but the beautiful bubble bursts, and I'm right back where I started. Where do I go from here? What power, if any, do I have to make things right?"

You can be certain of one power, that of choice. You can choose to turn your life in the opposite direction. You need not be strong about it. You need not know where you are going. You need have no security of any kind. You need not determine that you will endure in your choice, for at the beginning it is impossible. There are still too many negativities within you that don't want you to wake up.

You need only choose to turn, then keep choosing as many times as necessary. That is all you need do. And it is certainly something you can do. Then, as you continue to choose, everything is yours, just as turning toward a lovely sunset makes it yours.

Magnificent! If only you will grasp this! Do you see how you can now lay aside all your pointless duties, your false responsibilities, your artificial strengths? Do you see how you can be in love with life because you no longer fear it?

Choose to turn in the opposite direction. Do it now. Do it, and the whole universe belongs to you.

## *Steps in this chapter for becoming a new person*

1. Wish for newness more than anything else.
2. Walk the Mystic Path with quiet wonderment. It is a special type of energy.
3. You need never submit your integrity to anyone or anything.
4. We must walk beyond mere intellectual agreement to cosmic ideas to their total absorption.
5. When cosmic ideas are fully understood, they create a new man, a new woman.
6. Newness provides an amazing self-confidence. You are uninfluenced by anything exterior to yourself.
7. By daring to abandon shaky supports, you find yourself on the solid ground of Reality at last.
8. You can use any present troubles to make yourself a new person.
9. Do not try to create life-success. Merely let it exist in your awakened mind.
10. Choose to be a new person.

# 13

# Some Pleasant Surprises about Yourself

Many years ago a book published in the Arabian language swept over Europe to become the favorite reading of kings and citizens alike. Entitled *Hai Ebn Yokdhan*, it was written by a mystic and physician named Ibn Tufail, who lived in Seville, Spain. So great was the demand for *Hai Ebn Yokdhan* that it was translated into English, Spanish, French, German, Dutch.

What made it so fascinating to everyone? It aroused the sleeping powers within readers, shaking and guiding them toward inner release and employment of their mystical forces. The book told of a man who found himself all alone on a deserted island, completely on his own. Making up his mind to solve the secrets of both the spiritual and natural worlds, he went to work — and succeeded brilliantly. Without aid from people or books, he found within himself all he needed for the victorious life.

You have all the mental and psychic energy you need for a triumphant day, every day. But to avoid wastage, let's take an example of useless thinking. It is when people worry, "But what can I do about all my accumulated difficulties?"

Never forget this simple but remarkable reality: The more you walk toward the mountain, the more you walk away from the desert. This means you need attend only to where you are going, not to where you are or where you have been. As long as you are headed for the mountains, what slightest concern need you have for the scorched desert? The desert is not your home; the mountaintop is your dwelling place.

A tremendous gush of energy pushes you forward, once you realize that everything you do is done for your own sake. The ordinary man does not really see this. What little work he does is done from an annoying sense of required duty, or because it satisfies his imaginary image of being a sincere seeker. There is no energy in this; on the contrary, it is a burdensome drain on natural forces. The gush of fresh power comes from sighting that we are *actually working for ourselves.*

## You Have Abundant Energy Now!

Picture yourself surrounded by a number of small pools, each representing a different type of energy. A sign above each identifies them as Emotional Energy, Mental Energy, Sex Energy, Social Energy, Physical Energy, and so on. During the day you draw from each as you feel the need. You use Mental Energy to complete a business project, you draw from Social Energy to have a good time at a party.

The well-balanced person has plenty of energy to do whatever he wishes. Anyone wishing the energetic life must first aim at inner unity, which releases his powers.

Unity removes the cover on this pool, or that, making available the energy previously denied. It is useless to try to create energy by artificial means, such as trying to enjoy a party by being the witty clown. Energy flows from in to out, never from out to in.

When you grow tired of a certain activity, it merely means you have temporarily used up that particular pool of energy. When this happens, you should simply go along with nature to a different activity which calls upon another pool, permitting the previous pool to refresh itself. When tired of mental work, do something physical. When weary of entertainment that exhausts the emotions, turn to reading requiring careful thought.

You won't need to think about changing an activity; it happens by itself whenever a pool is exhausted. Just be aware of the signal and follow it. Although this is a natural process, conscious understanding of it provides release and relief. A businessman can abandon his hard drive without feeling that he is lazy. A tired mother can set the children aside for awhile without feeling neglectful of them.

Discouraged people say, "I know I'm supposed to try, but I've tried until I'm exhausted. I know I must persist, but it's been weary years. I'm like a man who persistently tries to open a lock with the wrong key."

True, nothing is more tiring than fumbling with the wrong key. That is why this book emphasizes the need for understanding basic psychological facts. With them our patient work pays profit.

Here is a psychological fact to understand: A weak person will try to drain the strength of a stronger individual. There are dozens of tricks by which the weak one will attempt to draw power to which he is not entitled: He may chatter endlessly, unload a sense of guilt through accusing another, boast, ask personal questions, and so on. Be alert to this. Refuse absolutely to let anyone drain your energies. At a certain point in your psychic development you can walk among the weakest of men and be the strongest of men.

Be very careful that you do not unconsciously assume that nervous tension is power. This is vital. Watch yourself the next time you work toward some goal. Look very closely to discover tense feelings and nervous thoughts whirling around inside. Do not let them deceive you into assuming that they are creative forces; they are not. They are thieves of genuine powers. As always, your awareness of their thievery is your first fine step toward casting them out.

"Half the time I forget why I am working on myself. It weakens my effort."

"What is your life like now? And how would you like it to be? See the contrast in the two. Keep the difference in mind. That energizes you."

## Why You Should Please Yourself

Remember, every cosmic fact has a thousand times more significance than appears at first. It is like following a narrow trail that leads to a beautiful valley. Recall our previous investigation of *time:*

The present moment is all there is; there isn't anything else. Reality is whatever thought, or feeling, or event we experience *now*. We may think about an unhappy past or hopeful future, but we think about them *now*. Yesterday and tomorrow do not exist except as this moment's memory or anticipation. To try to live in them creates illusion and conflict. Happiness is truly now or never.

"Confine yourself to the present." (Marcus Aurelius)

This is of overwhelming significance. Your day is never the same once you see it; all is magnificently transformed. You cease the vain attempt to run away from fear and sorrow and become aware of them as present experiences

— which magically removes them. No longer are you anxious toward your future, for you no longer insist that it conform to past pleasurable experiences — so every new second is lived completely and carefree. You see that there is really no choice but to live fully right now — and so strain and struggle fall away.

The man who sees this is like a sea bird whose wings are weary of the back and forth flight over the empty sea. He knows no alternative but to return to the mast of the advancing ship, and in so doing, finds the very restful progress he sought.

The facts that free us to live richly are often shocking to our smug ego-armor. None is more disturbing to some people than this one:

You must not live with a calculated motive of pleasing other people. Such motive is ego-centered; it expects some kind of reward. When the reward fails to come, as it often does, the so-called pleasantness turns to secret resentment.

There are dozens of solid reasons why you should seek to please yourself first, rather than others. Here are just a few:

*Only when you are genuinely pleased with yourself can you establish permanent pleasantness with others.*

*It maintains your health and integrity as a human being.*

*It relieves you of the tension involved in pleasing people who are incapable of being pleased.*

*Others sense the strength of your independence, which encourages their own development.*

*Because in your heart you know it must be done.*

It is an interesting psychological law: You must place yourself first, after which you have the strength and wisdom to please others properly.

"A great man is coming to eat at my house," wrote Emerson. "I do not wish to please him; I wish that he should wish to please me."

*Summary:* Please yourself, your real self.

## Move Out!

Picture a man living alone in a run-down shack in the middle of the burning desert. All around is dryness and desolation. His days are pointless and his nights are lonely. Every morning he ventures forth to find something interesting to do, but his day goes nowhere.

A friend calls to hear the complaint, "What's the matter with me? Here I am, a perfectly normal and intelligent human being making an effort to enrich myself. I start off every morning with good intentions, but find nothing. What's wrong?"

The friend replies, "Very simple. You start your search from the wrong place, the desert. You can't get water, or fruit, or friendship here."

"So what do I do?"

"Move. Change your headquarters."

"To where?"

"To the rich valley over the mountain. Then, all will be different. Everything depends upon where you are living *from.*"

"How do I know such a rich valley actually exists?"

"Go there for yourself."

"But I'm so used to this place. As miserable as it is, it's become a habit."

"Yes, that's your main problem. You prefer your comfortable misery. Shake yourself! Get going! Move Out!"

What an adventure awaits the man or woman who does this!

You see, *everything depends upon the psychological headquarters from which we live.* If we dwell in the desert of negative feelings and defeated thoughts, we then experience their barrenness. A man who frets over his financial affairs — regardless of what they actually are —

is living from a psychological desert. So is the woman who worries over her youth or beauty.

What kind of thinking gradually, but faithfully, moves us over to the bountiful valley? Examples:

*Genuine aid awaits you right now.*

*There is no problem without a solution.*

*No person nor event has power to harm you.*

*Your entire life can change magically.*

"Where am I living *from?*" Ask yourself that question. If you don't like your headquarters, you can move any time you like.

Break away. Don't tell anyone about it. Others will either smile tolerantly or mouth sanctimonious babble. Make your escape plans in secret. Never mind if you lose certain friends. You need to lose them and the sooner the better. In time you will find others who also have dared. They will be ten thousand times more valuable to you.

Half the battle is won when a man awakens enough to see that he does not live freely, but rather, lives as a slave to his own negative emotions and to society's tyrannical demands. That awareness sounds the battle cry of freedom.

Search out the truth for yourself. You are perfectly capable of doing just that. Don't believe something just because someone tells you it is true. Refuse glittering promises which have given you — as you well know — nothing but a broken heart. Stand on the integrity of your own mind. That is the only way in the whole world you will ever rest in inner tranquility in a troubled society. It is the sure way and the way you really want to walk.

*The only reason you do not do great things is because you timidly cling to small things. Will you let loose of small things and bear the uncertainty of having nothing for awhile? Do this and eventually you will do great things.*

## How to Melt Unhappy Feelings

There is a way to make unhappiness a thing of the past. It works every time, if you will but work with it.

If men and women could only see what negative feelings do to them. They are a terrible drain upon time and energy and health. They are thieves of your right to be a carefree human being.

By negative feeling, I mean an emotion causing distress. It might be gloominess, a feeling that life is pointless, self-dislike, hurt feelings, nervousness, anything painful. Try to search out your own particular negativities. That is fine self-responsibility.

Before supplying the three steps to dismissal, I want to add a personal note: I have spent many years in persistent exploration of these ideas, which resulted in definite discoveries. I want to pass them on to you in their simplest and most practical form. I know for a fact that your own persistent pursuit will give you the liberty of spirit for which you yearn.

Whenever you feel distressed:

**1.** Try to become fully aware of the negative feeling.

**2.** See that it is in *you*, not in exterior conditions.

**3.** Do not take it as part of your True Self.

Firstly, the moment you feel unhappy, you should stop and look at it. Just take a good look. Even though you are physically busy at office or home, mentally pause to become aware that it is there. This is more important than you can imagine. You see, you cannot destroy a negative feeling if you are unaware of it. It is like a rancher who cannot rid his range of roving wolves because he cannot find their den.

Secondly, realize that the distress is in you, not in anything exterior to yourself. No person has ever made you unhappy. No loss of employment, no shame or embarrassment, no failure, nothing outside you has the slightest power to disturb you. Negative feelings are *your* feelings. An exterior challenge may certainly arise, but *you react* to it. You unconsciously permit an exterior event to tell you how to feel. But you will do that no longer. You are tired of getting jerked this way and that, like a helpless puppet.

Thirdly, never, never, never take the negativity as part of the essential you, the True Self. It is not a part of your original nature, for that nature is free right now and always has been free. If you do not have this freedom, it is because you identify with the feeling, you react, "I am distressed." Having mistakenly said it, you suffer. Instead, see the negativity as a tiger walking through your mind, as entirely separate from you, not as a tiger housed within your mind. Whenever distress arises, say, "That painful tiger is walking through my mind but is certainly not a part of the essential me." Repeat this tremendous truth a thousand times if necessary, whenever you feel unhappy.

You have just covered information that might otherwise take you a lifetime to discover in the hard way. For your own sake, do things the easy way. There is no need for you to be unhappy about anything. And I mean *anything*. So work with the three basic steps. You will know what it means to live as a carefree human being.

## How to Regain Natural Liberty

"I want to be independent of other people. I mean, I don't like wanting something from them along with the fear that I won't get it. This is torture."

"Force yourself to act differently than usual. Notice your habitual behavior, then do the exact opposite. This isn't easy at first. Your deeply entrenched habits will scream in protest. Don't give in. Act toward people in an opposite way."

"Exactly how?"

"Suppose you habitually do lots of nice things for people. Stop it. Do the reverse. Let them be nice to you for a change. No, I am not advocating unniceness. I want you to pause in your usual efforts at niceness to observe your innermost motives for doing them. You may discover, for instance, a desperate need to be liked, which is pain. Your observation gradually frees you from this desperate bargaining. This is secret magic. Let people be nice to you for a change."

"What a relief *that* would be."

"Children know this secret. A child enters the room. Everyone enters his world; he won't enter yours. As adults, we can regain this natural liberty."

"But my show of independence might cause me to lose someone I desire."

"You must have great courage to escape this painful trap. You meet someone who is pleasant, say someone of the opposite sex. He or she makes you feel good, so you try to hold onto him or her. But something happens so that you no longer meet. You agonize. Try to see that, in reality, you are just as free of this person now as when you first met him or her. Tired of desperation? Then work with this."

Suppose you placed heavy blocks in front of a powerful jet airplane, then opened the jets full blast. What would happen? The airplane would shake itself to pieces. It would not be able to bear the contradictory forces. Man is like that. Loaded with power, but blocked by psychic contradictions, he is unable to speed forward into flight. He remains in a fixed place where he shakes himself to pieces.

To remove psychic blocks, ask yourself, "What would it be like if I acted and reacted opposite to my usual way? I usually get upset, so what would it be like if I simply did not? I usually shoot out an impulsively swift reply to a disturbing remark from another, so how would I feel if I dropped this habitual response? I am living anxiously, but what is it like to live without tension?"

Ask such questions over and over, putting as much understanding as possible into them. See that you may be wrongly assuming that a *familiar* response is the only possible response. It is not. The whole idea is to glimpse a fresh form of reaction to daily challenges. Along with your new response comes delightful self-command.

Why should you do this? Because you will feel better.

## Your Goal is Total Living

One effective way to get ahead is to examine carefully any new idea we feel inclined to resist. The reason for resistance is the ego-self's fear of its own destruction at the hands of a truthful idea. Go against your own inclinations. This does not mean that we gullibly accept anything that comes along. It means we courageously examine a new idea until it reveals itself one way or another, just as we might study a treasure map for authenticity.

Tell the truth boldly to yourself, disregarding the discomfort which will surely arise. Though unpleasant for the moment, your conscious pain, like taking a bitter dose of medicine, dismisses unconscious suffering from your day.

Now I must review one of the very worst enemies preventing you from living victoriously. The enemy is *pretense*. Pretense is always involved in unhappiness. Try to see this. Men and women pretend about everything. The ego-self is fantastically tricky. It even pretends that it is not pretending! Nothing cuts off happiness more than the false claim that it already exists within oneself.

The big mistake is self-deceptive labeling. A man is active, or successful, or educated and calls it happiness. It isn't. That is like placing a peach label on a can of sauerkraut and expecting a peach pie.

The Mystic Path gently but firmly calls upon us to stop pretending. We must willingly face the crisis of seeing that we are not really happy. We must stick with this shocking fact and not try to evade it. Stick with it, examine it, not with fear, but with curiosity. By so doing, we at last solve a great esoteric mystery: Conscious awareness of unhappiness destroys it forever. Remember, all unhappiness is unconscious, that is, we are unaware of how unhappy we really are. So become more conscious of the way you actually feel. Consciousness *is* happiness.

As pretense goes away, self-defeating compromise also goes. We compromise with people because we think we must do so in order to get what we need. But any need requiring compromise is false. You can expose it as false by refusing absolutely to compromise with anyone or anything. Yes, you may have to hold your breath and plunge into unknown waters, but that is how to be born anew.

"Be not the slave of your own past...plunge into the sublime seas, dive deep, and swim far, so shall you come back with self-respect, with new power, with an advanced experience, that shall explain and overlook the old." (Ralph Waldo Emerson)

Here is the way back: Place total living before intellectual gymnastics. That solves everything. Deep within, you know how to live fully; you have always known. You knew it in childhood before hypnotized people misled you. Whenever you don't understand life, dismiss your mind and live without straining to understand. Total living *is* understanding, just as you understand an apple by handling, tasting, eating. Why *ask* about an apple? Just eat it. It is for health and enjoyment. And so is life. We learn what life is all about when we dare to live simply, directly, without needing to know anything. This is not a paradox; it is a beautiful state.

## Two Things You Can Do

"How does all this connect with emotional aches, like dejection?"

"Dejection occurs when one suddenly sees through his

215

own play-acting. Pretense is a major feature of the false sense of self. A man pretends to others that he is strong and wise; he loses his wife or girl friend in a quarrel. This shatters his pretense and drops him into gloom. Dejection must periodically break through as long as we identify with the false self. But it becomes absolutely impossible when falseness is dissolved in insight. It is as impossible as it is for a non-existent man to have a headache."

We will never solve a single confusion, nor conquer a pain permanently, nor burst a point of pressure, until we see that all such problems originate in pretense-pictures of who we are. It is overwhelmingly necessary to think constantly and deeply about this. No matter where we go, regardless of all the books we read and lectures we attend, until we have at least a glimpse of this esoteric secret, we will miss the mark.

You are not who you think you are. You are someone entirely different. That someone is the person you want to be — sunny, healthy, without the slightest concern about tomorrow, just like a child.

Can a man honestly see that he is in psychological prison? That is the question. We cannot escape from self-imprisonment unless we observe it as a fact. Does he get upset when things go wrong? That is one cell of psychological prison. Does he harbor secret resentments and antagonisms? That is another. Is he bound by mechanical habits which he can neither break nor endure? Does he suffer at the hands of daily incidents? Is he afraid of himself? All this is what is meant by psychological jail.

No man or woman can enjoy life in this condition. Even his pleasures are surrounded by anxieties. He is like a prisoner in a real jail who plays baseball in the prison yard but who realizes that he will end up that night in the same cell. We can only enjoy the game of life when we are both consciously and unconsciously outside the wall.

There is a way over the wall. If we can become alertly

aware of our psychic imprisonment, that by itself moves us closer to freedom. The ending of unconscious imprisonment is the beginning of conscious liberty.

When faced with the seeming imprisonment of life you can do one of two things: You can sink in despair or you can laugh. Most people sink. You be different. Laugh. You have broken through.

## You Should Drift Comfortably

You should live like a man drifting comfortably downstream, letting the river turn in whatever direction it likes. Such a man drifts in perfect comfort and security as long as he does not fight the river, unless he insists that it should bend left instead of right. This profound secret for easy living is summarized in the New Testament with, "Resist not evil." When this esoteric truth infills a man he ceases to resist anything. He rests comfortably, regardless of the turns of life.

We do not spend enough time in just drifting through life without plan or purpose. We have it all figured out, and, if we find one minute of the day unfilled, we anxiously devise an artificial activity to get past it. That is the terror of the man who has not found himself; he is afraid to face his own seeming emptiness.

Don't dread to drift through your inner life; don't be afraid of having nothing to think about. Here is your very deliverance from all the strains and tensions of the day. An unplanned inner life will not harm your necessary activities in the exterior world, as a matter of fact, they will shine with new brightness.

You need not plan your inner day; it is already planned for you, and delightfully so. Be willing to drift. It is what you really want. A willingness to wander reveals the true nature of things, as Taoism teaches. By getting our rigid human plans out of the way we find, amazingly, that our life is lived for us. And we are glad at last.

"But I can't just drift through life."

"Why can't you?"

"A man must have a purpose, a goal."

"What is your purpose?"

"I don't know. It changes every day. I have never known what I want."

"Maybe the purpose of life is something entirely different from what you think it is. Have you ever considered that possibility? Maybe you are on the edge of a great secret."

"By drifting through life you don't mean irresponsibility?"

"No. You will want to take full responsibility for your family, and finances, and other everyday things. The point is to not live internally from fixed and habitual attitudes, but rather to be loose, flexible to change for the better. Then, a man becomes a better husband, father, citizen."

"But what *is* the purpose of life?"

"You can state it in several ways, but they all mean the same thing. The purpose is to find the True Self, to grow spiritually, to develop into conscious and awakened human beings. When we seek first the Kingdom of Heaven, all other purposes are added to us, like loving someone and being loved."

"I sense you are trying to tell me something of great significance, but I don't grasp it as yet."

"Welcome it. Let it come. It will."

## *Vital ideas in this chapter to think about*

1. Release your hidden energies by grasping the principles of the Mystic Path.
2. Remember your aim of self-transformation.
3. Please yourself properly.
4. Break away from limited living. You are capable of great achievements.
5. A carefree day can be yours.
6. Realize that there are new ways of reacting to life. Such realization is power.
7. Tell the truth boldly to yourself.
8. Do not strain to understand life. Just live.
9. A pleasant surprise of the Mystic Path is your newness as a person.
10. When you see what it means to drift comfortably through life, that is just what you do.

# 14

# How to Smash
# Barriers and
# Speed Ahead

People don't fail in their cosmic quest because they lack intelligence. The reason for failure can be illustrated by a case: A man living in an uncomfortable hut is told he has inherited a mansion, but, if he refuses to leave his hut, he cannot occupy his new home. He may insist on a guarantee that the mansion actually exists, but his only guarantee is to see and occupy the mansion for himself.

Cosmic growth requires that we *first leave the old*. We cannot occupy two places at the same time. Obviously, to get *there*, we must first leave *here*. This means we must take the first step — abandoning our habitual ways of thinking in order to make room for the new and powerful. To fly in an airplane above the storm, we must first leave the ground.

Growth comes by daring to risk more of the unknown than we are willing to risk. Dare it, venture it — and grow. Declare, "My known ways of thinking have brought me nothing but failure, so why cling to them? I dare to gradually detach myself from the old and the unworkable." Forget the difficulties, and confusions, and disappointments, for they are unimportant. Remember the only vital thing — the direction in which you are heading.

Confidently abandon yourself to higher truths.

Here is a heroic act!

What does it mean to confidently abandon yourself to something? It means you are completely unconcerned toward that something, that you don't even think about its reliability, just as a child abandons his welfare to his father.

Try it. Totally abandon yourself to higher truths.

There is no point in compromising. Compromise is a subtle thief of inner abundance. A spiritual principle is either true, or it isn't. So go all out. Be different from the millions of people described by Henry David Thoreau as leading lives of "quiet desperation." Dare to test things for yourself. It is a heroic business to personally experience a reality *as* a reality.

*Take no thought for tomorrow.*

Confidently abandon yourself to that.

*You can have everything you really need.*

Rest assured that you can.

*Strain and struggle are unnecessary.*

Live with it wholeheartedly.

*Total security comes to the enlightened man.*

Dare to prove it.

*You have inner wisdom for perfect guidance.*

Stand on that principle.

Factual knowledge of cosmic principles is not enough; we must permit them to change old life for new. The merely educated man knows the facts; the enlightened man lives them. The world has plenty of education; enlightenment is the sad lack.

## Dare to Think for Yourself

Everything depends upon how badly we want to escape our binding chains. We must have a determined intention to crash through the ill fictions that bar us from healing facts. We build strength for this by constantly plunging into psychological waters over our heads. We must meet, ponder, understand, and, finally, live advanced truths. That is what we now do.

There is a particular timidity that every seeker must meet and conquer. It is expressed, "But if I abandon my old ways, what will become of me?" Do not be afraid of what will become of you. Never mind the loss of your present ways. You may not see it as yet, but what will become of you is everything good and wonderful. Do not be afraid. Truth does not give us more than we can bear for the moment. It is gentle and patient. It allows us to rest on one level before urging us on to the next.

Great progress comes from the simple practice of breaking through the habitual self. The next time you find yourself self-absorbed, abruptly break this hypnotic state by deliberately turning your awareness to an outside object, perhaps a painting on the wall, or a tree bending in the wind. Notice the vast difference between the two states. In self-absorption, nothing exists to you except that state; therefore, it is limited, hypnotic. But, by directing your attention outward, you go beyond the cramped mind into a state of exterior awareness. Practice this from time to time. It turns you from a self-shackled person into a free and conscious individual. To wake up is everything.

It is all very simple. We can live in ego-centered hypnosis with all its fierce competition and hounding anxiety, or we can extinguish the ego-self and live peacefully. First, we must become as consciously aware as possible of our inner distress. Then we can attribute it to ego-centered living. Finally, we can work with life-liberating truths, such as the need for mental integrity.

Don't compromise with your own intelligence by asking other people what to do. They don't know any more than you. "I could not believe that I ought for a single moment to be satisfied with the opinions of another." (René Descartes) Dare to make up your mind about puzzling matters, even if you make a mistake. It is necessary to exercise your own mind, if you are ever to reduce and abolish mistakes. Don't let other people make mistakes for you; have the courage to make your own. A small tree cannot grow to full height, when sheltered by a large tree.

You must first learn to think for yourself. When reaching a certain elevation on the Mystic Path, you are relieved of all responsibility for thinking for yourself. Your life is thought for you. It is like wisely investing your money in a prosperous firm, after which you let dividends accrue effortlessly.

## Remember This Simple Rule

Anything you win with strain and struggle is shaky and impermanent. You will fear losing it. Notice how people worry over their prestige, and money, and friends. There is a superior way. There is a struggleless victory with rewards that you can never lose. They appear when we operate from the cosmic level, not the human.

Many people start down the Mystic Path to cosmic power by facing their own doubts about spiritual truths. It is either true that you need take no thought for tomorrow, or it isn't. If you think it isn't, you must courageously face your own doubts and plunge on from there. If it is true, which it is, and I know it is, then you will eventually experience the liberating fact that you need take no thought for tomorrow.

"I sense something magical in all this, but I'm afraid I still live in daydreams."

"Daydreams take the place of actual happenings, when a desire exceeds what we think we can get."

"I want genuine magic."

"It exists, but discovery can come only when we first abandon beliefs in false magic."

"What is false magic?"

"Looking for quick thrills and passing sensations. Arousing your emotions gives the illusion of life, but it soon vanishes, leaving you empty. It is like borrowing money. Sooner or later you must give it up. And what a dreadful rate of interest. You just can't afford it."

"I always come back to the question of what I should do to break through. Is there some simple rule to remember?"

"Say *yes* to whatever aids self-discovery; say *no* to whatever hinders it."

The Mystic Path winds upward, like a mountain road with many tunnels of various lengths. The traveler passes through the darkness of each tunnel to find himself on a higher level than before. Each tunnel represents a fresh crisis which must be daringly met. A man must not stand hesitantly at the mouth of a new tunnel and rationalize his reluctance by pretending that he is already on the other side. In spite of all contrary feelings, he must plunge into its unknown darkness and walk ahead until he comes out — as he always will — on the other side, a finer, happier, more purified human being.

What are these tunnels that the mystics urge us to pass through? Generally, they are anything stemming from our false self. Specifically, they are made up of prides, vanities, angers, envies, all negativities.

Constantly ask yourself, "What level is above this one?" This makes things different. Take personal problems for example. Problems are not solved by choosing between this and that. The very need to choose indicates misunderstanding. Problems are solved by outgrowing both this and that.

Buddha compared the world of men to a lotus pond. Some of the lotuses are deep in the water; others struggle to break the surface, while more are above, untouched by the pond. Every man and woman is at a different level of development, but all can grow upward.

## The One Sure Way to Bliss

How to grow?

Suppose you look out your window during a storm to see your neighbor rush from his home with some firewood and matches. To your amazement, he starts a fire, then miserably huddles over it in an attempt at warmth. You shout, "What are you doing?" He shivers and calls back, "Trying to keep warm. Can't you see the storm?" You reply, "Don't be foolish. Forget the storm. Just warm the interior of your home and stay there."

A neighbor would never behave like that in a real storm, but that is exactly what millions of men and women do when attacked by a psychological storm. One of the most widely known of all esoteric truths is that inward rightness corrects a man's exterior affairs. There is no sense trying to battle the exterior storm itself, for it is but an effect. When we are right within, things are right without. So there is but one place to remain and work — within our own system of conditionings, desires, impulses, imaginations. There is where we can work with endless profit.

"When will I stop paying the price for my false ideas?"

"When you get totally tired of paying. If you are living a second-rate life, it is only because you falsely assume it is the best you can do. You are somewhat tired of it, but you are still afraid to extinguish your wrong ideas, because you fear there is nothing else beyond them. There is, but you must dare to lose the old before finding the new. This is mystical law. Only an empty cup can be filled."

"Why don't weary people like myself break through?"

"It is not enough to feel weary of your life. Everyone feels that to one degree or another. You must take the initiative in breaking free. This does not mean to change your work, or residence, or anything else in your exterior world. It means taking a long and good look at your mental attitudes until you see them as the causes of your effects. As they change, your exterior world will be as different as if you had moved to Mars."

Yes, become utterly weary. Remain in that state until you see it completely. Do not cover it up with excitements or pretenses. That is like thinking that the bandage eliminates the wound. Simply become aware of how unhappy you are. Do not try to hide it. Your very awareness is the magic potion that changes weariness to bliss. You say you want a magical change in the way you live? This is it. I assure you that it is the one way and the sure way.

Perhaps you ask, "How fast can I change things?" The answer is, just as fast as you let your life be guided by mystical principles. People gamble to better themselves by switching things in their exterior world. When done without understanding mystical laws, they always lose, even if they think they win. When done with insight, they always win, even though on the surface they appear to lose. You cannot better *yourself* by getting something different on the outside for the simple reason that *you* are not a new career, or another spouse, or a different automobile.

Start today with this change: When faced with a difficulty, do not ask, "What should I do?" but rather, "What must I understand?"

## Unhappiness Exists Only in the Mind

Every man is struggling for something, but does not know what that something is. He even assumes, mistakenly, that he is struggling *against* something, perhaps human injustice or unlucky breaks. But beneath surface appearances, he is truly on a positive pursuit of his natural values of love, dignity, nobility.

He makes a great mistake in thinking he can regain these natural rights by attachment to and pleading with exterior attractions. Failing to perceive his Kingdom of Heaven within, he vainly seeks it in outer attractions. He is like a prosperous farmer standing by his wheat fields asking strangers for grain.

To make correction, here is a mighty mystical secret to ponder and practice: Learn to say silently to people and objects that *attract* you, "No, I will not give you power over me."

Do not shield yourself from the everyday events of life that you think are a threat to you. I refer to such things as contact with an unpleasant person or getting hurt when something turns out differently from what you wanted. Enter fully into the vastness of life, letting everything happen, while you quietly stand aside as a tranquil observer. Do not live like a tightly-sealed bottle of water tossed into the sea. Such isolation is fear and torment. Smash the bottle, mix with the sea, and you will know the oneness and immensity of life.

When you welcome a change, you call it variety and enjoy it. When you resist a change, you call it tragedy and suffer pain. Don't you see that it is your calling, your labeling, and not change itself, that makes the difference between joy and pain? Don't label changes. Call them neither good nor bad. Do not inject into them your personal attitudes and automatic feelings. Let them alone, let them be, and they will let you alone to be at peace.

A chief problem confronting the sincere seeker is his

inability to separate right ideas from wrong, to practice workable techniques instead of useless ones, to do what he can actually do, instead of attempting something which is yet beyond him. How can he meet this? He can start with a single, clear idea and gradually connect it with everything else. It is much like a lost hunter who heads for a distant but clearly observed farmhouse.

For instance, you must stop being a slave to your physical defects, and to your age. Stop it, and stop it right now. You have already paid a dreadful price. Any unhappiness you have toward them exists only in your mind. Rebel against your own false ideas that your years, or your physical construction, have anything to do with your happiness. They haven't a thing — if only you see it, if only you cease your unconscious bondage.

## A Valuable Technique for Awareness

"What do you mean by unconscious bondage?"

"For example, people feel unwanted, unappreciated. They yearn for others to come to them with surprises, gifts, phone calls, letters. They find great delight in unexpected pleasantries. But this is unconscious bondage; it keeps them anxious and frustrated. Awareness could free them."

"With all the pain caused by such negative emotions, why do we cling to them so stubbornly? I know people who actually *enjoy* depression. They can hardly wait to tell you all about it."

"Yes, it is a strange feature of human nature that people harmfully love negativity. It gives one a false sense of aliveness, of vitality. Take hatred. Although it burns up the hateful one, he gets a perverse pleasure from it. This proves that all self-harm is unconscious; that is, a man doesn't see what he is doing to himself. No one *consciously* hurts himself. This is why the goal of your life should be more consciousness."

"But we are also attracted to positive feelings, like

gentleness."

"True. A man's better self wants them, but is usually smothered by his accumulated negativities. As he works, his desire for the harmful goes down, and attraction to the good goes up, like elevators passing in opposite directions."

We have covered self-awareness so much in these pages that it is good to review. Let's take the simple instance of exterior awareness. As you finish reading this line, become aware of the expression on your face. Is it tense, relaxed, sad, curious — just what? Take a mental look and see. What are your facial expressions when you chat with the family, as you go about your work? Try to be conscious of what they say, how they change, what inner feeling prompts their exterior appearance.

Also, alertly but casually watch the expressions of others. You will find it much easier to study theirs than your own. Did that man laugh at the joke mechanically, not because it was funny, but because it was expected of him? Did that woman tighten up defensively to a criticism? Just notice the passing drama.

This is an excellent start for developing intuitive understanding of your moods and actions. It awakens you. You can then plunge deeper and deeper into your self-structure, until you finally become the person you want to be — someone who knows what it is all about.

Everything counts for gain when we are cosmically awake. Nothing counts, unless we are awake. No enjoyments last, no successes satisfy, no gains have meaning unless accomplished in a state of wakefulness. "Only that day dawns to which we are awake." (Henry David Thoreau)

If you would spend each possible minute and every spark of energy to become aware of what it means to be an awakened human being, you could wave a magic wand over your day.

But do not think you must immediately grasp the full

nature of this richer life. Do not let the gap between where you are and where you want to be discourage you. All you need is the desire to go on. You need nothing but a sincere desire. Forget all else and walk ahead.

## How to Get Right Results

Look at the calendar on the wall. Notice the date. This is the date you possess the understanding you need. Today. But you must bring them close. Suppose the conductor of a symphony orchestra tried to direct his musicians while standing at the back of the auditorium. Having no control at that distance, the musicians would not know what to do. Each would play different compositions at various tempos, producing discord. But as the conductor comes increasingly closer to his proper position, the musicians see what is expected of them. Disharmony disappears.

The musicians are your imbedded understandings and insights. As you take your proper position before them, they follow your slightest command, producing the music you want to live by.

We might as well turn into stones if we are not going to do this. That is right; we might as well be as senseless as stones if we are not going to feel as free as a lilting melody.

Take the power of making demands. The power of demand is dynamic in the human system. Rightly used, it liberates; wrongly used, it imprisons.

Cease making demands upon anyone or anything exterior to yourself. Such demands are always accompanied by fear and pain, which makes them wrong for you. Have you noticed how unhappy you are when demanding something?

Do not think this will deny you what you need. Quite the opposite. By eliminating artificial needs, it makes room for genuine ones. Do not think you will be unhappy if you do not get what you demand. Think very deeply for a moment. Demanding things from the exterior world is an endlessly agonizing process. Even when you get what you want, you are really no happier than before; you have merely covered up your anxiety for a few minutes. And then you are tossed right back into the pain of the next demand.

If you want opposite results from what you have been getting, take the opposite course: Turn all demands inward. *Demand your own power.* Insist that your mind work for you, not against you. Demand that you stop being so afraid. Command your habits to be what you wish. Demand constant and sincere work toward your own deliverance.

Anyone can make loud demands upon people, and government, and society. If you don't want to be just anyone, ponder these ideas.

The world desperately needs bold individuals who connect their understanding with their powers. By boldness I don't mean public arrogance and loud talk springing from cunning egotism. We need men and women who are not afraid to be themselves, who bravely battle for inner conquest, those with a glimpse of the New Life which impels them to turn their backs on shadows and their faces to substance.

When you attain a degree of self-transformation, you need not tell others about it. If you really have, they will know. You spontaneously send out radiations which they intuitively sense. The light in them responds to the light in you. Neither you nor they need have any connections with exterior or man-made forms of religion or education. It is all a matter of inner essence. India's enlightened teacher, Sri Ramakrishna, likened it to the way a lotus blossom attracts bees. Because the honey is there, the bees fly to it.

In this higher state you can help others in the only way that counts — not merely by doing something for them, but by being someone who truly understands. To see how this

231

is so we can recall a previous point: Through self-work, the mystic has found his own way home, and so can aid others. It is as if he stands on top of a high hill and looks down on the prairie where a confused humanity wanders about. Knowing where the Path starts, he calls down. But how many, do you suppose, will look up and listen?

## The Beauty of Disillusionment

To be disillusioned is a wonderful state to achieve, a marvelous breakthrough into sunlight. Do not think of disillusion as a sad thing. "We think this state is terrible. We are mistaken. It is there that we find peace, liberty ...." (Francois Fénelon)

Disillusionment with yourself must precede enlightenment. If you are disillusioned, I am very glad for you, for now there are great possibilities. Do you feel that nothing you know can fulfill you? Great. You are preparing a psychic emptiness, which can be filled with something making sense at last. You are ready to leap from the frustrating known to the emancipating unknown, magnificently beyond your present self.

Tired of trying to believe in something? Good for you. You can now let something believe in you.

It is especially splendid to get disillusioned with people, most of all, your best friends. No, not in cynicism and bitterness, for these are still prison cells consisting of your own defensive attitudes. You don't want emotion-charged attitudes toward lost people; you want clear discernment of their lost state. In such clarity there is total calmness and command.

There is something quite fascinating, I assure you, in being so disillusioned toward others that you are left without a single friend, or counselor, or authority to lean upon. Your very awareness of the inability of others to help you forces you to look, at last, toward your only genuine source of strength, the kingdom within. It is as if a weary wanderer, refused lodging, turns to leave, and in so doing, sights his inherited castle.

The whole idea is to see ourselves and others as we presently are, for upon the ruins of our disillusionment we build a castle we can actually occupy. You build swiftly when you make these insights of French philosopher La Rochefoucauld your own.

*We assume the look and appearance we want to be known for, so that the entire world is a mass of masks.*

*We offer praise only that we may benefit from it.*

*Only strong natures can be sweet ones. Those that appear sweet are usually only weak, and may easily turn sour.*

It is severely damaging for anyone to pretend possession of a virtue which, in fact, he possesses only in imagination. If a person thinks he is already loving, he cannot go on to find the genuine article. Not only that, but if we think we have bread in the cupboard, when in fact we don't, we will be hungry when we need bread. Such imagination is a dangerous foe of freedom, and far more difficult to detect than one might suppose. Negative imagination is a major cause of human hypnosis. It must be detected, and abandoned. Start with honest Self-Observation. Review the technique for this from Chapter 2.

La Rochefoucauld's insight represents a certain stage toward cosmic consciousness. It is one in which you no longer idolize people by attributing qualities and virtues to them which they don't really possess. A person at this stage realizes that his admiration of others is merely a subtle projection of self-admiration. Seeing through himself, he sees through others. This brings great relief, for you are never nervous toward anyone you really understand.

Disillusionment is nothing else but seeing the false *as* false, and is therefore an advanced mental condition.

## How to Reverse Your Life

People miss the point of daily existence entirely. They assume that life is complicated, when it is really themselves who needlessly make it so. They are like a starving man who won't eat dinner until he first knows the cook's name, whether the bread was baked in a brick or steel oven, and how many times the soup was stirred.

Don't ask, "Does God really exist?" Ask, "How come I have so many stupid headaches?" Don't wonder, "Does the future hold security or dread for me?" Wonder, "Does it make any sense to be miserable this day?" Don't inquire, "Why can't I find the satisfaction I need?" Inquire, "Why don't I just live without bothering with so many questions?"

Living from the True Self is the great answer.

Man is like a tree wanting to push itself to the sky. As it grows upward, the various branches take over to insist that they can reach the top quicker and easier than the trunk. But all they do is drain energy and retard growth. The man who grows surely toward the sky is the one who refuses to go along with such false branches as sensation-seeking and egotistical desires.

The True Self carries us upward. Here is where genuine self-knowledge enters the picture.

Lack of self-knowledge leads to self-defeat. A man decides to better his life in some way. Fine. But since he does not know what his true interests are, he does the wrong or impulsive thing. He ends up even worse than before, because he has now added another burdensome false branch. In turn, that creates an anxiety which impels him to once more shoot off in a wrong direction. He is caught in the frightening vicious circle which grows smaller around him every year.

Genuine self-knowledge reverses the whole process. He sees what is genuinely good for him. He lives more and more from his True Self in which there is self-victory. The man is skyward bound.

There is a simple but sure test as to whether or not we are living from truth: To the degree that we are, we are free from conscious and unconscious suffering caused by living from illusion. Millions of people do not use this test to advantage, even though Christ could not have made it plainer: "You shall know the truth and the truth shall set you free."

It is just as simple as that. If I know the truth, I am free of my pains. If I realize that no one can really hurt me, no one hurts me. If I actually see that in spite of a terrified imagination, all is well with my basic self, my imagination loses power to terrify me.

To see that we suffer because of blurred vision toward life is no reason for despair. It is cause for a joyful mental leap. Now knowing what is false, we have made room for what is true.

We can have the comfort of knowing the truth, when we are willing to go first through its discomfort. Endured self-exposure is the cure. If we are willing to see that we are not living from our true nature, but from an invented self, our very awareness abolishes the painful invented self. We then live in comfort from our true nature.

Would you like a grand summary of what you must do? *Be true to your own nature.*

## *How to make swift progress*

1. Don't hesitate to abandon yourself to higher truths.
2. Break through your habitual self. Beyond it is the new world you seek.
3. Trust your own intelligence.
4. Know that victory without struggle exists. It comes with cosmic consciousness.
5. Say *yes* to everything that moves you forward, *no* to whatever blocks progress.
6. Challenge yourself to mount up to higher and higher levels of self-realization.
7. Your progress will be as speedy as you permit guidance by mystical principles.
8. Psychic wakefulness is a magic wand.
9. Be glad for disillusionment. It indicates healthy advancement.
10. Be true to your own nature.

# 15

# Daily Power
# Along The
# Mystic Path

This chapter is especially designed to aid you in making the most of this book, of the Mystic Path and of yourself.

You have a right to know the truth that sets you free. But you must courageously claim this right and not timidly hand it over to someone else. For you to know, *you* must know. You will then also know what it means to be secure and serene.

There are some special challenges faced by the man or woman wanting to escape to the awakened life. If understood, everything goes much smoother. For one thing, you may have to work alone a good part of the time. You may have no one with whom you can discuss things. Never mind. Even that is part of your adventure. Just keep working as best you can. The higher the hurdle, the higher your leap.

You will find none of the self-glory offered by worldly success. Our whole task is the exact opposite — to destroy the agonizing need for self-worship. You may not win public applause, but what you win will be ten-thousand times more glittering. And it lasts for eternity.

Do everything you can to help yourself. What wonderful opportunities surround you! Go through your day with inner reflections about mystical principles. Observe yourself as often as possible. Establish a regular reading program. Remember your aim of inner transformation. Remind yourself that there is a fantastically new way to live. Be good humored toward everything that happens to you.

Yes, you can be cheerful even when things look cheerless. Take the attitude, "It is my heroic adventure to call the bluff on this negativity." Apply this to every difficulty — fear of poverty, anxiety toward yourself, confusion of mind, everything whatsoever.

If you ever feel bogged down in your studies, just remind yourself that it is possible for you to become an entirely different person, that you can reverse the direction of your life this very day. No fact is more important to think about than this. And it is just the beginning. The best is yet to come.

Let go. Don't hesitate to just let go, even if it frightens you for now. Do not think, or plan, or contrive on the inner affairs of life. Leave your mental plannings where they belong — in the external matters of home and office. Let your inner life flow naturally and easily; it will carry every external affair along with it, leaving you carefree.

"He who lives in the True Light and True Love, has the most precious, best, and worthiest life that ever was or ever will be. Therefore it cannot but be loved and treasured above any other life." *(Theologia Germanica)*

## *Vital questions and answers*

QUESTION: *Why do the objects of my happiness cease to satisfy after a few days or weeks?*

ANSWER: Because you cannot be happy with *something*; you can only be happy. When your happiness has an object, whether a person or a worldly goal, it is an insincere flirtation that always wears off. True happiness has no object. Does sunshine need an object to shine upon in order to be warm? No. Sunshine *is*. Happiness *is*.

QUESTION: *I want to walk the Mystic Path, but wonder whether I have enough courage.*

ANSWER: Start with what little you have. It will grow. It takes courage to realize that you can no longer live in the old way, especially when you cannot, as yet, see that a new way exists. It wonderfully exists, but you must walk the royal road without demanding the security of foreknowledge.

QUESTION: *Please supply an example of how unawareness causes grief.*

ANSWER: Never sacrifice your integrity to another in order to get something from him or her. It is completely unnecessary. Once you clearly see that you are sacrificing yourself, you will stop.

QUESTION: *How does mysticism connect with modern psychology?*

ANSWER: Mysticism includes psychology but goes far beyond it. As an example of their blending, take hatred. Both urge us not to suppress or fear our hatreds, but expose them to the purifying light of awareness. This is called growth into mental maturity by psychology. Mysticism says it is a fine step upward toward Love.

QUESTION: *I want to give these principles to my children. How can I best proceed?*

ANSWER: What an opportunity you have for doing them good! Center your teaching — but, especially, your *example* — around a few basic principles. Teach them self-responsibility. Show them there is nothing to fear. Encourage them in the old-fashioned virtues of honesty, decency, simplicity. Repeatedly point out that they need not be defeated by anyone or anything. Teach all this as the grand fact of life that it certainly is.

QUESTION: *What does the Mystic Path say about human immorality?*

ANSWER: The basic immorality is refusal of truth, to insist upon living from the false self. All human immorality springs from this. Most people connect immorality with observable faults, or with sex. But the terrible immoralities are the cunning ones hiding behind masks of morality, such as exploiting people while pretending to help them.

QUESTION: *The Mystic Path says we must cease to invent emotional excitements. Won't life become boring?*

ANSWER: It will become the exact opposite. You will have genuine excitement that won't swing over to boredom, as is now the case. This new kind of excitement cannot be described, but you can experience it for yourself.

QUESTION: *Why don't your lectures on mysticism include psychic phenomena like telepathy and flying saucers?*

ANSWER: If a man suffers from heartache, what difference does it make whether flying saucers exist or not? Let's stick to the point. People are always looking for miracles. The great miracle is a changed life.

QUESTION: *Mysticism says that the birth of the new self cuts us free from guilt and shame of past follies. How?*

ANSWER: You clearly see that the follies were committed by a confused and foolish self who was not the real you.

QUESTION: *What qualification do we need for teaching mystical principles to others?*

ANSWER: It might be helpful to really know what we are talking about. Otherwise, we are like a man without an airplane who invites his friends for a ride in the sky.

QUESTION: *What is the very heart of successful human relations?*

ANSWER: Through honest Self-Observation, we see ourselves as we really are. That enables us to see others as they really are, not as we want them to be. This psychological insight enables us to deal wisely with others. For instance, we will not extend affection to those whose psychic slumber makes them incapable of understanding it. Such people will assume that our affection is weakness, and they scorn it.

QUESTION: *You said that the natural love of the True Self is within everyone. Why doesn't it express itself?*

ANSWER: It cannot do so because the individual fears rejection, or because he wrongly prefers hostility, or because his ego-defenses are so high.

QUESTION: *Can't we just leave our psychic wounds to the healing of time?*

ANSWER: Time of itself doesn't heal; your mind must see things differently. By using your mind properly, you can leave a painful experience behind you at once, with no emotional wounds whatsoever. Think what this means!

QUESTION: *How can I become a more self-aware person?*

ANSWER: Just sit down in a quiet place and watch yourself. Notice the thoughts that stream through your mind, observe your emotional moods, be aware of your physical posture, notice whether you are tense or relaxed. Just be alert to everything possible, including the fluttering of a drape or the sound of a passing car.

Be aware of everything within you, and without. Also, practice this while performing everyday tasks in the home or office.

QUESTION: *Why do you place so much emphasis on Self-Observation?*

ANSWER: Because of where it takes you. You can get to the place where you are no longer involved in inner or exterior disturbances. You will merely observe them, just as if they were happening to someone else.

QUESTION: *How can I end my nervousness?*

ANSWER: By understanding one of the most subtle of all fears. It is so cunning that few people ever destroy it through conscious awareness. It is the fear of nothing happening. We become nervous when we feel that we should be accomplishing something but don't know what it is. So we usually invent foolish activities. Don't be afraid of nothing happening in your life. What peace it brings.

QUESTION: *I get upset every day over things that happen. How can I prevent this endless distress?*

ANSWER: We never get upset over what happens. Never. We get upset because of preconceived ideas as to what we think *should* happen, what we *want* to happen. When our preference clashes with the reality, we get hurt. Rid yourself of all preconceived ideas as to what should happen. You are then at peace whatever happens. Work with this mystical truth.

QUESTION: *What if a man has his own ideas about life and personally disagrees with the principles of mysticism?*

ANSWER: It is not a question of personal agreement or disagreement. The only question in the whole wide world is whether or not he wants to be a whole and a happy human being. Our personal viewpoints cannot achieve this. Only the Truth can set us free, and Truth is not a matter of personal viewpoint.

QUESTION: *You said that a hypnotized man has no real choice to live as he wants. It seems to me that most people live the way they really want.*

ANSWER: A man living from his false self can only choose between two negativities, for example, to show his anger or to hide it. But he cannot choose not to be angry in the first place. Can a hawk choose to behave either as a hawk or as a dove? No. He must behave inwardly according to his present negative nature, though he may disguise it from others. Incidentally, the self-discovered man also has no choice, but in a different way. There is nothing to choose between. When you are really happy, need you choose between happiness and unhappiness?

QUESTION: *Please explain human cruelty.*

ANSWER: It is characterized by two features. First, a cruel person gets a strange sort of exhilaration, a false sense of power, by hurting another. Secondly, he doesn't see how cruelty destroys his psychic self. If he saw cruelty as self-ruin, he would stop in horror. All evil, including cruelty, is unconscious. It is done in a hypnotic state of unawareness.

QUESTION: *What is the cause and cure of social miseries like war, and crime, and political hypocrisy?*

ANSWER: The cause is personal psychic illness, which means every individual must take personal responsibility for his recovery. But how many want to do this? They prefer to treat symptoms, not causes. Hypnotized people prefer ego-serving activities, such as making lofty speeches and championing social causes. A small-town grocery clerk in Maine or Nebraska with a personally pure life diffuses more psychic health than a thousand politicians or laws.

QUESTION: *Suppose I do something that hurts someone. From the mystical viewpoint, how should I handle it?*

ANSWER: By not falling into ego-centered guilt or shame. This only doubles the problem. Try to see that your hurtful behavior sprang from the false self which takes unhealthy pleasure in hurting others. Don't identify with the behavior. Dissociate your behavior from your True Self which cannot hurt anyone.

QUESTION: *I need clearer understanding of what is meant by non-awareness.*

ANSWER: You are seated in a restaurant having dinner. A friend approaches from behind and taps you on the shoulder. You jump a mile. You jump because, while in your self-absorbed thoughts, you were unaware of anything outside those thoughts. The sudden tap on the shoulder exploded your mind away from self-centeredness. As awareness expands, all your senses are more alert.

QUESTION: *Why do you emphasize that we must work intensely upon ourselves before trying to help others?*

ANSWER: If there are two sick people in a hospital room, neither can help the other get well. If one recovers, he can pass on his own health in service to the other. Enormous harm is done by ill people who think they can heal others. Their attempts are merely an evasion of their own need for health. If you tell them this, they get angry.

QUESTION: *I'm very much interested in the idea that we are free of anything that we don't identify with, that we don't take as a permanent attachment.*

ANSWER: You should be! If you don't identify with youth, you will enjoy older years. When you refuse to identify with your career, you will be completely unconcerned if it falls apart. If you don't identify with crowds, it is impossible to ever be lonely. Don't identify with food, and you remain as slender as a reed.

QUESTION: *Why does sex cause so many problems?*

ANSWER: Sex never causes problems. It is compulsions,

and imaginations, and false guilt that do damage. When there is a clear mind, there are none of these and so no problems whatsoever.

QUESTION: *Should we discuss mystical truths with others?*

ANSWER: Discuss them only with those who show definite and persistent interest. Don't try to give them to people who don't want them. You can establish or join a Mystic Path Study Group with like-minded people. There is considerable value in group discussions.

QUESTION: *Is it difficult to grasp the principles of the Mystic Path?*

ANSWER: The word *difficult* has no meaning when you want something badly enough, for example, in studying for a profession. You simply do it to win the prize. In the same way we must want freedom from tension, genuine confidence, and so on. Then there is no difficulty. As a matter of fact, it becomes a highly enjoyable adventure.

QUESTION: *Please summarize man's entire problem.*

ANSWER: He clings to his false self, which he takes as his life, but which is actually destruction; and he rejects his True Self, which he takes as his enemy, but which, in reality, is his eternal life.

## Your Special Plans

Use this section to win extra enrichment from your reading and studying. Certain ideas and techniques of the Mystic Path are sure to have special meaning for you. Write them down in the blank spaces provided, noting the page where found. It deepens your understanding to state a mystical truth in your own words. For example, you read that life is governed by a number of beneficial laws and principles. You can write, "I am aided by harmonizing with the basic principles of life." Review your comments from time to time.

## Daily Power Along The Mystic Path

1. _____
   _____ Page _____

2. _____
   _____ Page _____

3. _____
   _____ Page _____

4. _____
   _____ Page _____

5. _____
   _____ Page _____

6. _____
   _____ Page _____

7. _____
   _____ Page _____

8. _____
   _____ Page _____

9. _____
   _____ Page _____

10. _____
    _____ Page _____

11. _____
    _____ Page _____

12. _____
    _____ Page _____

13. _____
   _____ Page _____

14. _____
   _____ Page _____

15. _____
   _____ Page _____

16. _____
   _____ Page _____

17. _____
   _____ Page _____

18. _____
   _____ Page _____

19. _____
   _____ Page _____

20. _____
   _____ Page _____

21. _____
   _____ Page _____

22. _____
   _____ Page _____

23. _____
   _____ Page _____

24. _____
   _____ Page _____

## Gems along the mystic path

- Truth itself is the only unifying factor on earth. We are separated from love with others to the same degree that we are separated from Reality. We are in communion with others to the same degree as our closeness to Reality.
- Let nothing stand in your way.
- You can react toward anything that happens to you in a way that retains your happiness — if you really want your happiness more than anything else.
- Suffering exposes our fakery. This is good. By exposing our fakery it provides the opportunity for freeing ourselves from its pain.
- The process of self-development can be described as the stripping away of layer after layer after layer of all that is false.
- Go to incredible lengths to save yourself.
- We do not suffer because we fail to fulfill a false desire. We suffer because we possess the false desire.
- Try to see how much you are at the mercy of other people's whims, and see how intensely you dislike it. This is the first stirring of liberty.
- Refuse to live like others. You then escape the unhappiness of others.
- Life is real only when we are.
- You have succeeded in life when all you really want is only what you really need.
- When you have nothing to do, become aware of yourself.
- By discovering yourself in the Here and Now, you automatically establish yourself in the There and Forever.
- Do not sacrifice long-term benefits for immediate sensations of pleasure.

249

- To be chosen, we must choose to be chosen.
- Unhappiness occurs when a desire for a certain result clashes with what actually results. The one man in a million — the always happy man — is the one who examines his desire, rather than the one who blames results.
- Fear is caused by our insistent clinging to the false self. As we become conscious of this, our fears fade fast.
- Every time you gain insight into a new truth, you are a bit stronger than before.
- Here are two sides to the same mystical coin: No one on earth can do you good except yourself; no one can harm you except yourself.
- Those who endure will be sure of themselves. Nothing can ever take away this certainty.
- Our suffering is trying to tell us something.
- The test of genuine spirituality is this: How spiritual can we be without anyone knowing about it?
- Take the viewpoint that you walk the Mystic Path to discover what is true and what is not.
- Don't be discouraged over anything. Turn every difficulty into increased determination for the light.
- You can walk beyond fear.
- There is no such thing as sad days or happy days. There are only sad people or happy people.
- It is a fantastic situation. The only thing that stands between us and buoyant happiness is our own unconscious resistance to it.
- If the ideas by which we live bring distress, the only sensible thing is to methodically exchange the unworkable principles for effective ones.
- The two shallow substitutes which people unconsciously take as happiness are activity and acquisition.

- Don't postpone happiness.
- Learn to do what you really want to do, not what you feel compelled to do by inner compulsion or by social custom. Our conscious awareness of these chains frees us at last.
- Be gentle toward yourself.
- If we work on ourselves when things go right, we will know what to do when things go wrong.
- Everything can be different.
- Self-liberation can begin by getting weary of our mechanical efforts to be good. By sensing the falseness of compulsive goodness, we track down the real thing.
- Never relax your guard against self-deception.
- Our aim is to get ourselves out of our own way.
- Make it your aim in life to be aware of psychic self-imprisonment and to escape it.
- We cease to suffer when we cease to identify with suffering.
- One of our greatest enemies is secret resentment. Freedom begins as we become conscious of it.
- There is no adventure in life as great and as wonderful as discovering the New Life.
- The test as to whether or not you have rejoined your True Self as yet is this: You would not exchange it for anything in the world.
- The Mystic Path changes your future into what you want it to be.
- If we really want to know the Truth that sets us free, we will be led to the teachers and books of help.
- You were not meant to be unhappy.
- At this very moment, we are creating our tomorrow.

- You never go wrong when you place your True Self before your attitudes. And, remember, they are two entirely different things.
- There is something very appealing about decency.
- To change what you get, you must change who you are.
- One ounce of personal spiritual experience is worth tons of hearing and reading about the experiences of others.
- Don't be offended by the Truth. Love it above all else. Your love will be returned. It is the Truth that sets us free.

*Notes*

## About VERNON HOWARD

\*\*\*\*\*\*\*\*\*\*\*\*\*\*\*\*\*\*\*\*\*\*\*\*\*\*\*\*\*\*\*\*\*\*\*\*\*\*\*\*\*\*

Vernon Howard was born in Haverhill, Massachusetts on March 16, 1918. When he was a boy his family moved to California where he lived for many years. He began writing and lecturing there on spiritual and psychological topics. He eventually moved from Los Angeles to Boulder City, Nevada where he lived and taught for many years. In 1979 he founded New Life Church and Literary Foundation.

From 1965 until his death in 1992 he wrote books and conducted classes which reflect a degree of skill and understanding that may be unsurpassed in modern history.

 *Human Behavior Magazine* once said of him, *"Vernon Howard is probably the clearest writer on these subjects in the English language."*

His warmth and refreshing sense of humor made him a delightful subject for interviews, talk shows and articles. In 1983 Michael Benner of station KLOS in Los Angeles, California said, *"Vernon Howard is one of the most powerful speakers I have ever interviewed. He has an uncanny ability to cut through the fluff and puff and jolt people into seeing who they really are. At times humorous and gentle, at other times demanding and forceful, Vernon holds the record for generating responses to our KLOS talk shows. Not everyone likes his message, but I can't imagine anyone turning him off."*

Vernon Howard broke through to another world. He saw through the illusion of suffering and fear and loneliness. In *The Esoteric Path to a New Life* MP3 Compact Disc there is a marvelous interview with Vernon Howard. Also included in this album is the booklet of the same name, which will give any new student a great introduction to Vernon Howard's teachings.

Today more than 8 million readers worldwide enjoy his exceptionally clear and inspiring presentations of the great truths of the ages. Libraries, bookstores, health food stores and church bookshops all over the country sell Vernon Howard books, booklets, audio, video and more. His material is widely used by doctors, psychiatrists, psychologists, clergymen, counselors, educators and people from all walks of life.

All his teachings center around one grand theme: *"There is a way out of the human problem and anyone can I find it."*

## About NEW LIFE FOUNDATION

New Life is a nonprofit organization founded by Vernon Howard in the 1970's, for the distribution and dissemination of his teachings. It is for anyone who has run out of his own answers and has said to himself, *"There has to be something else."* These teachings *are* the something else. All are encouraged to explore and apply these profound truths — *they work!*

The Foundation conducts classes on a regular basis throughout Arizona, Colorado and Southern California. They are an island of sanity in a confused world. The atmosphere is friendly, light and uplifting. Don't miss the opportunity to attend your first New Life class.

*For details on books, audio and video,*
*ongoing classes, banquets and much more,*
*call, write, fax, e-mail or visit our website at:*

## www.anewlife.org

*Headquarters*
**NEW LIFE FOUNDATION**
**PO Box 2230**
**Pine, Arizona 85544**
**(928) 476-3224**
Fax: (928) 476-4743
E-mail: info@anewlife.org

## Tell a friend!